The Panizzi Lectures
1996

Previously published Panizzi Lectures

BIBLIOGRAPHY AND THE SOCIOLOGY OF TEXTS
by D. F. McKenzie (*1985*)

ENGLISH MONARCHS AND THEIR BOOKS
by T. A. Birrell (*1986*)

A NATIONAL LIBRARY IN THEORY AND IN PRACTICE
by K. W. Humphreys (*1987*)

DAPHNIS AND CHLOE:
THE MARKETS AND METAMORPHOSES OF AN UNKNOWN BESTSELLER
by Giles Barber (*1988*)

THE DUTCH AND THEIR BOOKS IN THE MANUSCRIPT AGE
by J. P. Gumbert (*1989*)

ERASMUS, COLET AND MORE:
THE EARLY TUDOR HUMANISTS AND THEIR BOOKS
by J. B. Trapp (*1990*)

THE ENGLISH BOOK IN EIGHTEENTH-CENTURY GERMANY
by Bernhard Fabian (*1991*)

HEBREW MANUSCRIPTS OF EAST AND WEST:
TOWARDS A COMPARATIVE CODICOLOGY
by Malachi Beit-Arié (*1992*)

THE MANUSCRIPT LIBRARY OF SIR ROBERT COTTON
by Colin Tite (*1993*)

MUSIC, PRINT AND CULTURE IN EARLY SIXTEENTH-CENTURY ITALY
by Iain Fenlon (*1994*)

MAPS AS PRINTS IN THE ITALIAN RENAISSANCE
by David Woodward (*1995*)

The Panizzi Lectures
1996

The Introduction of Arabic Learning into England

CHARLES BURNETT

THE BRITISH LIBRARY

First published 1997 by
The British Library
Great Russell Street
London WC1B 3DG

Cataloguing in Publication Data
A catalogue record for this title is
available from The British Library

ISBN 0 7123 4545 0

Designed by John Mitchell
Typeset by Bexhill Phototypesetters, Bexhill-on-Sea
Printed in England by Henry Ling (Printers) Ltd,
Dorchester, Dorset

Contents

Preface

THE FOLLOWING LECTURES are based primarily on the manuscripts in the British Library. They are not meant to treat the proposed subject exhaustively, but take the form rather of an extended essay. By dealing with the material in chronological order it fell out, almost by chance, that the three lectures dealt respectively with monastic and cathedral schools, private tutors to the nobility, and the early universities. And yet it is a story of continuities, in successions of masters and pupils, of manuscripts and their copies, of ideal systems of learning which determined translation programmes over longer periods. As an essay the text is necessarily selective. More could have been said, for example, on the position of Paris in the story, on the importance of the Augustinian houses as centres of learning, on the role of intellectuals in government administration, on the condemnations of Aristotelian and Arabic philosophy, and on the discovery of Greek learning, in which John of Salisbury and Robert Grosseteste played a leading part. The substantial literature written in Anglo-Norman, Middle English and Hebrew is almost entirely neglected. The omissions reflect partly the areas of ignorance of the writer, partly the fact that others have written more fully and more competently on the neglected areas. However, two points must be observed about the title of the lectures. First, they are concerned only about the *introduction* of Arabic learning, not the reaction to, or subsequent development of, this learning. Hence they go no further forward in time than the period of the last medieval translations of Arabic philosophical texts into Latin, made by Hermann the German (d. 1272); the Arabic-Latin translations of the Renaissance are another story. Secondly, the term 'England' is not meant to exclude the Celtic areas of Wales, Scotland, Ireland and Cornwall, but rather encompasses the society of the British Isles in the eleventh to thirteenth centuries which was characterised by several languages and several cultures – among which Arabic should be included. It just happens that the intellectual centres in the British Isles during this period were on what is now English soil. Finally, emphasis has been placed on the enjoyable side of this learning as manifest in the playful anecdotes of masters and pupils, and the verses and jingles in which the learning was couched.

It remains to express my indebtedness to past and present scholars. It is no coincidence that the title recalls the chapter on 'The Introduction of Arabic Science into England' in Charles Homer Haskins's *Studies in the History of Mediaeval Science*, a book which Peter Dronke *sub sidere fausto* put into my hands when I wished to find a topic for my Ph. D dissertation. Charles Haskins and Peter Dronke showed the way, but other lode-stars have been Richard Hunt, Marie-Thérèse d'Alverny, and Richard Southern. Among those present who have helped, in many different ways, are Julia Barrow, Marion Campbell, John Carey, Oliver Gutman, Max Haas, Dag Nikolaus Hasse, Tzvi Langermann, Patrick McGurk, Raymond Mercier, Nigel Ramsay, Rodney Thomson, Tessa Webber, Geoffrey West and Paul Williamson. The staff of the Bodleian Library, the Warburg Institute and the Wellcome Institute have gone out of their way to provide photographs on time, and I thank them for permission to reproduce some of them here. I am also grateful to the Passmore Edwards Museum, the President and Fellows of Trinity College, Oxford, and the curators of the GPA Bolton Library in Cashel, for kindly allowing me to use photographs of their manuscripts. I regret very much not being able to recreate through the written word the singing of Clare Woods or the perfumes of the Dar al-Taqwa. Above all I am grateful to the trustees of the Panizzi Foundation for giving me the opportunity to prepare these lectures, and to Elaine Paintin, and the staff of the manuscript reading room, the photographers and the

Publishing Office of the British Library for their practical and spiritual support in bringing the lectures and the publication to fruition.

Abbreviations:

Adelard of Bath	*Adelard of Bath: An English Scientist and Arabist of the Early Twelfth Century*, ed. C. Burnett, Warburg Institute Surveys and Texts, 14, London, 1987
BGPM	*Beiträge zur Geschichte der Philosophie (und Theologie) des Mittelalters*
PL	Patrologia latina.

All manuscripts are from the British Library, unless otherwise indicated.

I

The Books of King Harold

In a mid-thirteenth-century manuscript from Wales we read, at the end of a text on chiromancy:

> There was in Britain a certain religious recluse called Hilaricus to whom God in His grace revealed through the message of an angel these signs on the hand which would benefit men and women. It happened that his brother was burdened by an illness. To save him, Hilaricus, devoted to God, bent his knees to the ground, extended his hands to heaven, and prayed that the Lord might reveal to him a clear sign of the recovery or death of his brother. The Lord therefore fulfilled his desire. For, rising from his prayer, he saw in front of him a marble statue of this kind, on which he noticed that a right hand of a man and a left hand of a woman were sculpted in which the above-mentioned signs were indicated.
>
> One should know that a certain natural art was discovered by a certain philosopher, Eadmund, who was previously a Saracen and was called Manean, but Master Adelard translated this art from Greek into Latin.[1]

Here we have the legend of a revelation to 'Hilaricus'; a conversion from Islam to Christianity entailing the change of an Arabic-sounding name ('Manean' perhaps for 'Ma'mūn') to a typically Anglo-Saxon name;[2] and the location in 'Britannia' – in this context probably referring to the Celtic domains of the 'Brittones', the common name for the Welsh in this period.

All this is legend. There is no evidence that chiromancy came from the Arabs; Adelard of Bath (ca. 1080–1150) did not translate from Greek; and the vision of the two marble hands is clearly modelled on visions of the statue of Hermes Trismegistus holding the Emerald Tablet in alchemical literature. However, relics of St. 'Hyldracus' were donated to the college of secular canons that the Anglo-Saxon King Harold Godwinson founded at Waltham.[3] Adelard wrote a work on hawking in which he said that he got his information from the experience of present-day hawkers, and 'from the books of King Harold'. In another version of Adelard's text the source is said to be a book 'of the good King Edward' (presumably the Confessor).[4] The manuscript that contains the chiromancy begins with a calendar with Welsh saints, and some uncomplimentary remarks about the defeat of Harold by 'William the Bastard of Normandy'.

Unfortunately I cannot substantiate from other sources a legend that Arabic learning formed part of a pre-Norman 'golden age' of Celtic or Anglo-Saxon philosophers. Nor can we recover King Harold's or King Edward's books.[5] Nevertheless, the Welsh Marches, Adelard of Bath and Waltham Abbey will figure quite prominently in our story.

It begins in the late tenth century in the Iberian peninsula. In Córdoba, the Umayyad caliph, al-Ḥakam II al-Mustanṣir (961–76), was establishing his kingdom of al-Andalus as an intellectual counterweight to the eastern caliphate of Baghdad by amassing an enormous library and attracted the foremost scholars to his court.[6] One result of this was the resurgence of mathematical and astronomical studies, associated with Maslama al-Majrīṭī (d. 1007) and his school. Maslama revised for the meridian of Córdoba the Indian astronomical tables arranged by al-Khwārizmī for Baghdad in 830 AD, and added notes to the Arabic translation of the classical work on the geometrical constructions that lie behind the operation of the astrolabe, the *Planisphere* of Ptolemy (2nd century AD). Al-Majrīṭī and his school became famous for their astrolabes and texts on how to make and use them. But to the astronomical tables of al-Khwārizmī, al-Majrīṭī added tables especially for astrological calculations.[7] The same al-Khwārizmī had introduced calculation with Indian numerals into the Arabic-reading world, and it is likely that his text on the subject was brought to al-Andalus at the same time as his astronomical tables. All these texts are concerned with *practice*: the use of Hindu-Arabic numerals for astronomical calculations, and the use of astronomy for astrology, medicine and weather forecasting.

The size and opulence of tenth-century Córdoba far outstripped any city in the Latin West, and the contrast between the scientific cultures of al-Andalus and Latin Christendom was just as extreme. It is perhaps not surprising then that Islamic doctrine concerning the science of the stars, along with other cultural artefacts, should overflow into its nearest Christian neighbour, Catalonia. It is here that we find, already in the late tenth century, the earliest references to chess pieces, the earliest representations of Hindu-Arabic numerals, and the earliest Latin astrolabe: an instrument probably constructed by an Arabic maker but inscribed by a Catalan scholar.[8] It is here, too, that, in all likelihood, the first corpus of Latin texts on the practical side of the science of the stars was put together from Arabic and Latin sources. This corpus consisted of texts on the astrolabe, on astrology and on astronomical tables.

For the astrolabe we have writings on its construction and use, and miscellaneous chapters on measuring heights and depths and distances with the instrument (i.e., surveying).[9] Ptolemy is regarded as the originator of this material. In the field of astrology the corpus included an elementary introduction to astrological principles, followed by texts on the characteristics of men born under each of the lunar mansions, the effects of planets in the zodiac signs, judgements from the hour that the client approaches the astrologer and the hours of the planets, and from the numerical value of the letters of the name of the client and of his mother. This collection of texts may be called the 'Alchandrean corpus' because its first text is attributed to 'Alchandreus philosophus'.[10] This complements the only Latin work on astrology which was being copied in this period: Julius

Firmicus Maternus's *Mathesis*. Finally, for astronomical tables, there is the *Preceptum canonis Ptolomei*, which is a crude translation made from Greek in 536 AD, of tables for the movement of the Sun and the Moon, together with instructions for use, which include information on how to draw up a horoscope.[11]

There are two intellectual frameworks into which this corpus fits. The first is the practical science of computing and surveying. In the Latin West the calculation of the church calendar (the *computus*) required considerable mathematical skill, and it was the *computistae* who first embraced the new texts from Arabic.[12] The texts gave practical instructions, but this did not prevent certain individual scholars from pursuing mathematical investigations beyond what was strictly necessary for the church, or from exploring the theoretical – even mystical – sides of the question. This has a parallel in the Arabic world in which many of the astronomers were by profession *muwaqqitūn*, i.e., those appointed to determine the exact time of the New Moon and of the daily prayers.[13] These early texts must be considered in the context of the monastery rather than the court.[14] The second framework is that of the quadrivium: the sciences of arithmetic, geometry, music and astronomy which Boethius had described as a 'four-fold' ('quadrivial') path to the understanding of things.[15] We shall see examples of these astronomical texts being assimilated into both frameworks.

The *Preceptum canonis* was of Greek origin. The other texts, however, are all based on, or incorporate, Arabic material. Passages of a text on the astrolabe by al-Khwārizmī have been identified in the *Sententie astrolabii*.[16] The theory and names of the lunar mansions in the Alchandrean corpus are also Arabic, as is some of the other astrological material in the collection.

All these works, with the exception of the *Preceptum canonis*, exist in several forms which were often transmitted together in the manuscripts: a crude Latin version, with many Arabic terms left in transliteration, and the recasting of the same material into a more literary language, often more than once, culminating, in the case of the works on the astrolabe, with the scientific corpus of Hermann, the lame monk of Reichenau (1013–54).

The astrolabe texts and the *Preceptum canonis* were promoted in the late tenth and early eleventh centuries in two Benedictine monasteries on the outskirts of Orléans: St-Benoît of Fleury and St. Mesmin of Micy, the abbeys respectively of Abbo (abbot from 988 to 1004) and Constantine (deacon and then abbot from 988 until 1121). The connections between Fleury and England, especially through the monastery of Ramsey in the East Midlands, where Abbo had been *scolasticus* ('school-master') in 986–8, are well-known.[17] Of the corpus I have mentioned, however, up to now only the text of Greek origin, the *Preceptum canonis*, has been shown to have come into the hands of English scholars through this Fleury connection. For, the earliest manuscript of these canons is Harley MS 2506 of ca. 1000 AD, which was written either at Fleury or at Ramsey and decorated by an English scribe.[18] However, we can trace another route by which texts from this corpus arrived in England.

From Fleury and/or Micy the texts on the astrolabe and the *Preceptum canonis* reached Chartres where they could be found, until it was destroyed in the Second World War, in Bibliothèque municipale, MS 214. Their presence there is probably due to Fulbert, bishop of Chartres from 1006 to 1028, who maintained close connections with Micy, and who wrote his own notes on the Arabic terms used in the astrolabe texts and on the Arabic names of the stars. He put the latter into the form of a poem, which must be the earliest example of verse with Arabic words in the Latin language. Since, as we shall see, verse became a popular medium for Arabic learning in England, it is worth recording it here:

Abdebaran Tauro, Geminis Menkeque Rigelque
Frons et Calbalazet prestant insigne Leoni;
Scorpie, Galbalagrab, tua sit, Capricornie, Deneb,
Tu, Batanalhaut, Piscibus es satis una duobus.[19]

Ad-dabarān is prominent in Taurus, *mankib* and *rijl* (*the shoulder and leg of the Twins*) in Gemini,
The forehead and *qalb al-asad* (*the heart of the Lion*), in Leo.
Yours, Scorpio, is *qalb al-'aqrab* (*the heart of the Scorpion*); yours, Capricorn, *dhanab* (*the tail*).
You, *baṭn al-ḥūt* (*the belly of the Fish*), are enough for both Fishes.

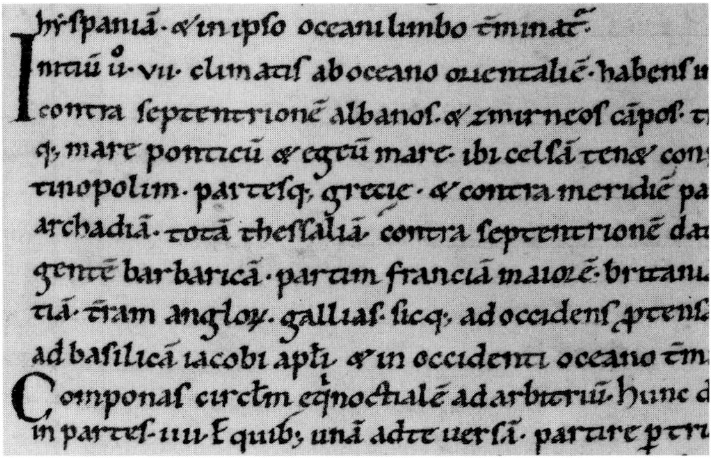

FIG. 1. Add. MS 17808, fol. 84r. The end of *De utilitatibus astrolabii* with the mention of Great Britain and St. James of Compostella, followed by the *Compositio astrolabii* of Ascelinus.

The same collection of texts that is found in MS Chartres 214 also occurs in an eleventh-century manuscript which forms part of codex 283 in Corpus Christi College, Oxford. There are reasons to believe that both manuscripts were copied in Chartres, and that the Corpus Christi manuscript was brought to England in the early twelfth century; for there are notes in it concerning Winchester and St Albans, and it had become the property of St Augustine's, Canterbury, by the fourteenth century.[20]

Two manuscripts add the Alchandrean corpus to the astrolabe texts: Munich, Bayerische Staatsbibliothek, clm 560, and British Library, Add. MS 17808, both of the eleventh century. The first of these is considered to have connections with Fleury.[21] The second includes no indication of its medieval provenance. The nineteenth-century list of contents are written in French.[22] However, it has the same selection of astrolabe texts as MS Corpus Christi 283. Its astrolabe texts are even more similar to those of the twelfth-century manuscript Avranches 235,[23] which passed from the Abbey of Bec to that of Mont St-Michel, and

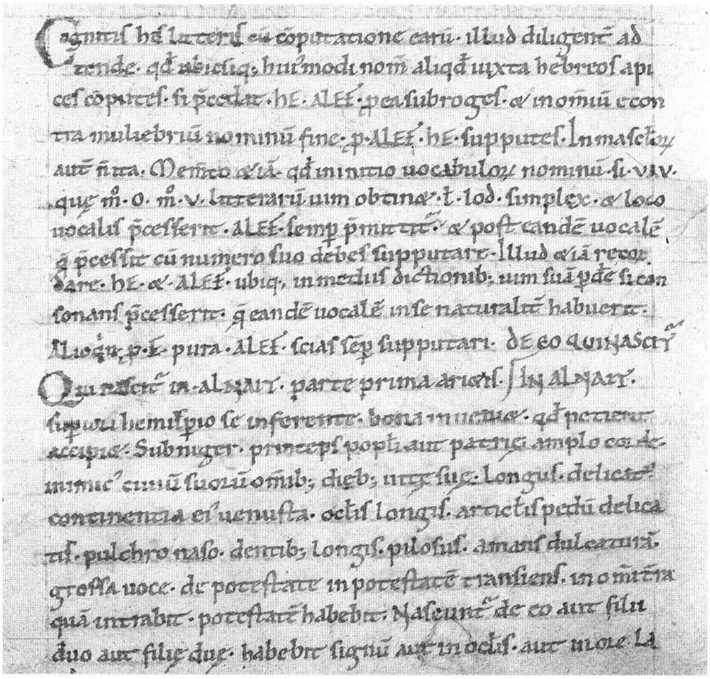

FIG.2. Add. MS 17808, fol.90v. A typical example of the kind of simple astrology which is characteristic of the Alchandrean corpus. One converts the letters of the name of the client and his mother into numbers (here it is specified that the name should be written first in *Hebrew* letters), and, having added up the numbers, one counts the same number of signs round the ecliptic circle, starting from the ascending sign, and one makes a judgement according to the nature of the sign that the number reaches. Below this is the beginning of the section on the lunar mansions. The first constellation that the Moon 'resides' in after leaving the first degree of Aries is *al-naṭḥ*, i.e., 'the butting (of the Ram)'. Amongst the characteristics of the man born under this mansion are, that he will have a beautiful nose, he will be hairy, he will like to eat sweets (*dulcatura*), and will be powerful; two sons or daughters will be born to him. He will live for 24 years, but if the constellation is kind, for 80 years.

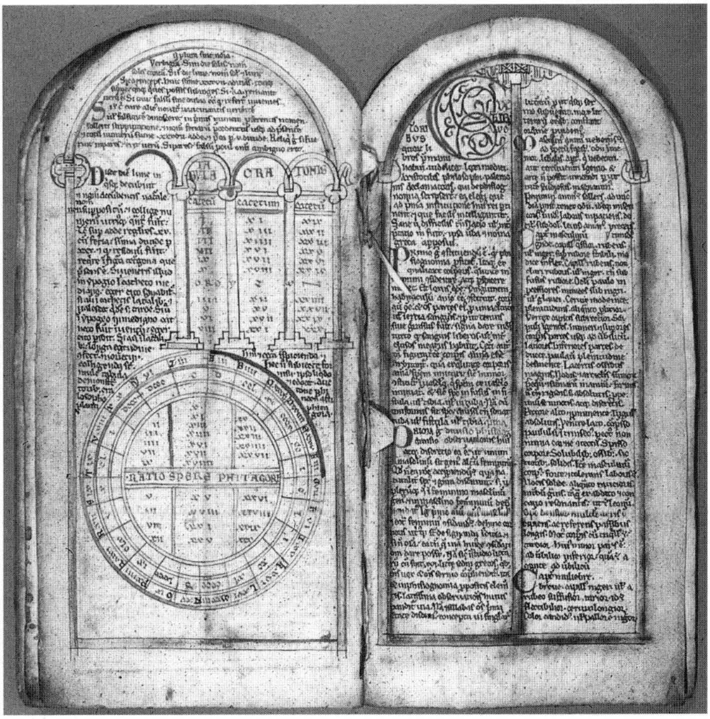

FIG.3. Wellcome, MS 21, fol.7v–8r. The end of the *Liber Alchandrei*, and an example of the 'Sphere of Pythagoras'. The shape of this twelfth-century manuscript (whose decoration suggests an Anglo-Norman context) imitates that of a writing tablet.

which included the earliest copies of the Arabic-Latin translations of Adelard of Bath. Only these three manuscripts contain the text on the construction of the astrolabe by Ascelinus of Augsburg, addressed to Constantine of Micy[24] and they must all belong to the same Anglo-Norman context.

Add. MS 17808, written entirely in one hand, is a manuscript of 'new' texts on the quadrivium. It starts with music: the new, practical, way of teaching the Gregorian chant, invented by Guido d'Arezzo (his *Micrologus* of 1026–32), with associated

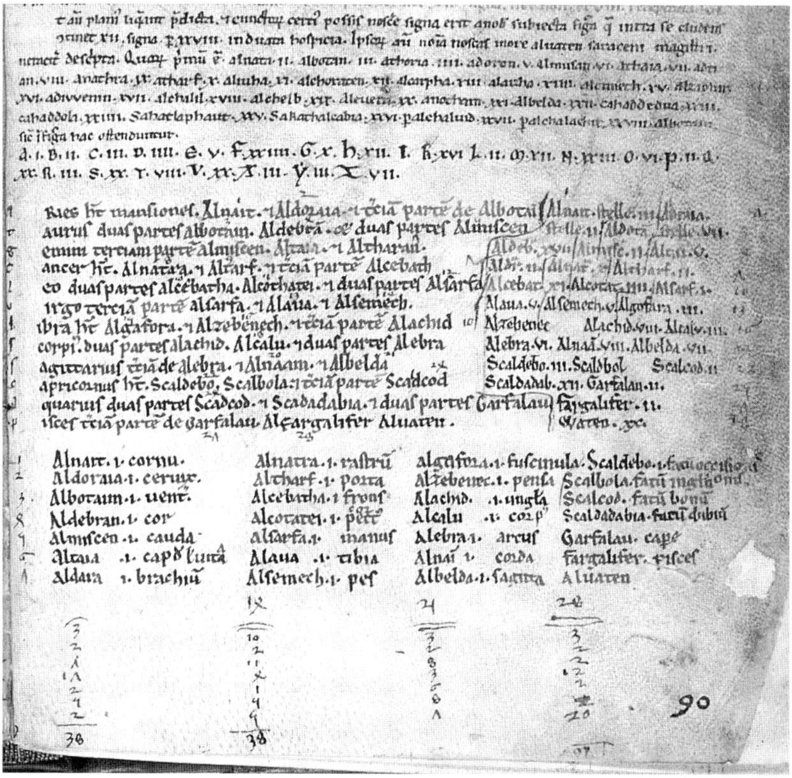

FIG.4. Sloane MS 2030, fol.94r. A chapter on lunar mansions from the Alchandrean corpus, beginning 'De celi spera continente .xii. signa necnon .xxviii. receptacula . . .' including a reference to a Saracen master: '. . . hospitia. Ipsorum autem nomina noscas more aluaten saraceni magistri veraciter descripta. Quorum primum est alnata .ii. albotan .iii. athoria . . .', followed by the numerical values of the letters of the alphabet and further lists of the lunar mansions.

tracts; an abacus text, for 'practical geometry', to which we shall return; and the texts on the science of the stars. These are the *De utilitatibus astrolabii* under the title *Regulae ex libris Ptolomei Regis*, and *De compositione astrolapsus*. These are the earliest of the literary redactions of the crude astrolabe texts translated in Catalonia, and are probably the responsibility of the translator of those crude versions. They are followed by the *Compositio astrolabii* of Ascelinus, and the *Liber Alchandrei Philosophi*, headed 'Mathematica Alhandrei Summi Astrologi'. On fol. 88v the scribe has added some mnemonic verses:

> Oriens, meridies, occidens, septentrio sunt ista climata mundi
> Ignis, aqua, aer, terra, mundi sunt hec elementa.[25]

The Alchandrean corpus had a brief success in England. Part of it survives in a curious diptych-shaped manuscript in the Wellcome Institute.[26] The renown of this early corpus of texts on the science of the stars is probably best indicated by the fact that William of Malmesbury, in indicating the scientific eminence of Gerbert d'Aurillac, compares his work with the most important texts in astronomy and astrology of his time, referring to Julius Firmicus Maternus's *Mathesis*, and to two of the parts of our corpus: the astrolabe texts attributed to Ptolemy, and 'Alhandraeus in astrorum interstitio'.[27]

Add. MS 17808 and Avranches 235 also show the heritage of Chartres, for they include some didactic verse by Fulbert of Chartres: this time on the duodecimal divisions of the pound ('libra' or 'as'),[28] a subject treated in abacus texts. The work on the abacus in Add. MS 17808, however, points to another heritage. For the author, a certain 'Bernelinus Junior of Paris' states at the beginning of the text that the procedure he is describing was invented by Gerbert, and developed in Lotharingia.[29]

Gerbert d'Aurillac (d. 1002) was a contemporary of Abbo of Fleury. Politically, the two were enemies – the one upholding the rights of the bishops, the other that of the monasteries – and they never mentioned each other. But both were interested in the quadrivium, Abbo probably as an adjunct to his computus studies, Gerbert, as a *scolasticus* at Rheims, where he eventually became archbishop. As a very young student Gerbert went to Vich in Catalonia to study the quadrivium. This is just the time when the corpus on the science of the stars was coming into being, but it is difficult to attribute to Gerbert the early diffusion of these works. Rather, he popularised a bizarre kind of abacus, which became part of the curriculum in quadrivial teaching for the next 150 years. This is called the 'abacus with *apices*'. It worked in this way:

Like abacuses throughout the world it had columns for units, tens, hundreds, thousands etc. But whereas in the common abacus the same number of counters or beads is added to columns as the number of units one wants to represent, in the 'abacus with *apices*' one uses counters with the requisite unit marked on them; the mark is called an 'apex'. So, one has nine heaps of counters marked with the numbers one to nine. This kind of abacus was probably never used by merchants or in the Exchequer. It was, rather, a teaching tool, and it is in the context of Gerbert's renowned teaching of the quadrivium that his pupil Richer mentions an 'abacus with 17 columns and 1000 counters made of bone'.[30]

It is often assumed that Gerbert took the abacus from the Arabs, and his sojourn in Catalonia provided the occasion for this. This statement is found in William of Malmesbury,[31] but earlier testimonies and Gerbert's own words confirm that neither did Gerbert discover the abacus, nor was the 'abacus with *apices*' an invention of the Arabs. For Gerbert is merely credited with renovating the study of the abacus, which was being pursued at the same time by some of his contemporaries, including Abbo of Fleury.[32] Both Gerbert's and his contemporaries' works on the abacus, however, do not discuss the instrument itself, but only the methods of calculating on it. It is claimed that the only 'Arabic' element is the use of Hindu-Arabic numerals on the counters, and that this is a later development. Since the counters are individually numbered, Roman numerals are inappropriate, because they are composed of varying numbers of letters. It is impracticable, for instance, to inscribe on a small counter 'V I I I I', the more common way of writing the Roman nine. A system in which numbers were represented by single symbols was preferable. But such a system was already available: i.e., the Greek alphabetical numerals which we find in computus works. On the oldest Latin astrolabe we find letters of the Latin alphabet used as numerals (A = 1, B = 2, C = 3, etc.),[33] and other attempts at Latin alphabetical numbering occur sporadically in

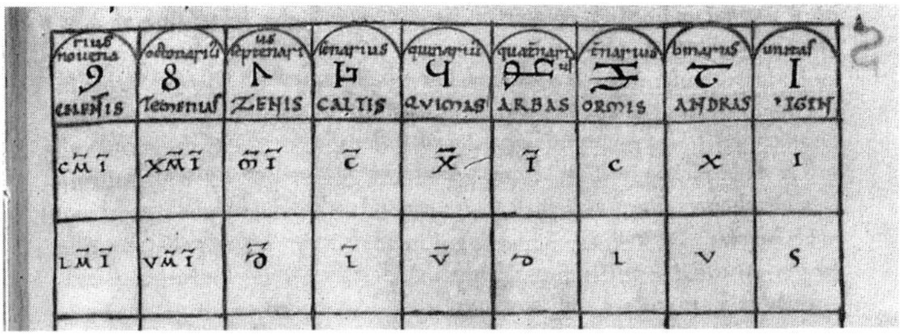

FIG.5. Harley MS 3595, fol.62r. Abacus numerals (reading from right to left – the Arabic way): 'igin, andras, ormis, arbas, quimas, caltis, zenis, temenias, celentis'.

Latin manuscripts,[34] but none of them caught on. Someone, somewhere, had the idea of using Arabic numerals, and calling the counters by names which are garbled (or dimly remembered?) versions of these numerals. One can recognize 'arbas' as the Arabic 'arba'a' (= 4) and 'temenias' as the Arabic 'thamāniya' (= 8); (see Fig. 5).

The Arabic element may, however, go beyond the mere forms and names of the numerals. A counter for zero is included. This is not necessary on an abacus in which one would simply leave a column empty. But in pen-reckoning, in which one does not have columns indicating the decimal places, a zero is necessary to 'hold the place'. In fact, what the 'abacus with *apices*' does is to represent graphically what happens in pen-reckoning, using Hindu-Arabic numerals (see Fig. 6).

Calculation with Hindu-Arabic numerals, as we have seen, had been described by al-Khwārizmī, and a hint of it occurs as an addition in two manuscripts of Isidore of Seville's *Etymologies*, written in the North of Spain in the late tenth century: 'We must know that the Indians have a most subtle talent and all other races yield to them in arithmetic, geometry and the other liberal arts. And this is clear in the 9 figures with which they are able to designate each and every degree of each order (of numbers). And these are the forms.' A row of Hindu-Arabic numerals follow.[35] What is strange is that it took another 150 years for

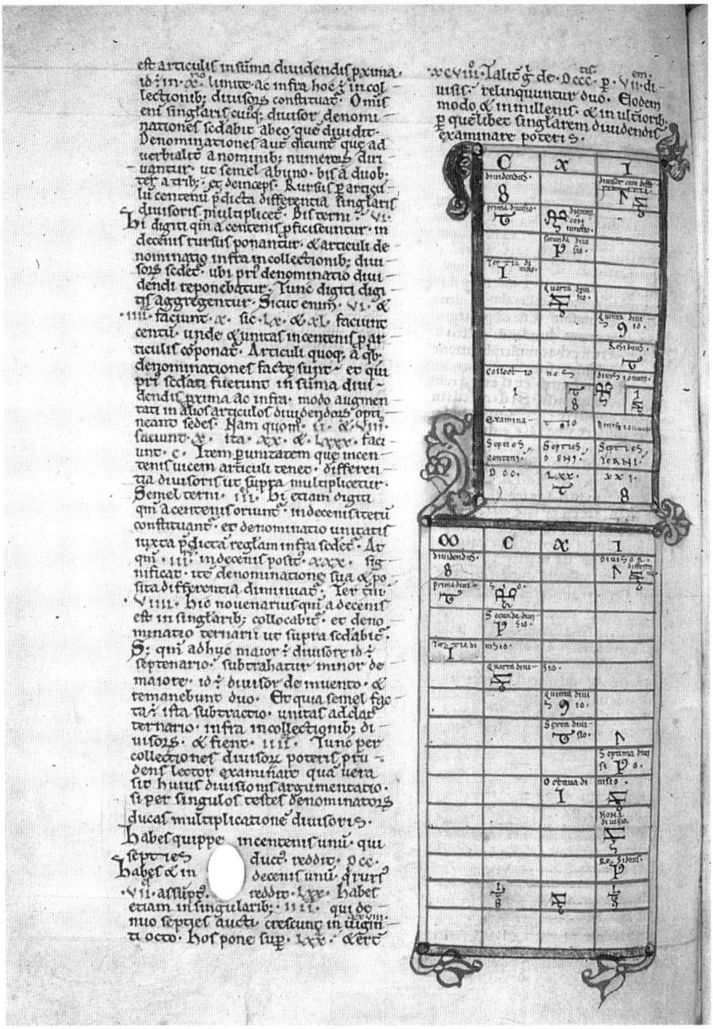

FIG.6. Bodleian Library, Auct. F.1.9, fol.56v. This shows the calculations of 800 divided by 7 and 8000 divided by 7.

pen-reckoning with Hindu-Arabic numerals (the 'algorism') to start being used by Latin scholars. One reason for the preference for an apparatus such as the abacus, however, is that, as Richer in his biography of Gerbert makes abundantly clear, the teaching of the quadrivium was teaching by means of *instruments*, not by means of writing: rhythmomachy for arithmetic, the abacus (and chess!) for geometry, the monochord for music, and celestial spheres and hemispheres for astronomy.[36] Many reasons may be adduced for this, such as the scarcity of writing material, the desire to differentiate the quadrivium (about *things*) from the trivium (about *words*), and the ability of three-dimensional instruments to represent the work of God who created the world by number, measure and proportion.

The earliest abacus text in which the Hindu-Arabic numerals on the counters are fully integrated into the work is that of Bernelinus. Bernelinus is described as being 'of Paris' but states at the beginning of his text both that knowledge of the abacus results from 'certain seeds, as it were, briefly and subtly sown by Gerbert', and that one should seek out the Lotharingians for knowledge of the subject, since, as he himself had experienced, they are most adept in it.[37] The implication is that he was a student in Lotharingia, where he would also have picked up the music theory that he wrote about, but all details of his bibliography remain uncertain.

In Lotharingia, the heartland of the empire of Charlemagne, we see the flowing together of several interrelated currents of learning: first the teaching of the quadrivium by Gerbert in Rheims; then the pupils of Fulbert, including Adelman of Liège, and two scholars, Raoul of Liège and Ragimbold of Cologne, who met each other in Chartres while working with Fulbert and wrote a series of letters to each other in ca. 1020–25 concerning a mathematical problem, in which they mentioned an astrolabe. And finally, the works of Hermann, the lame monk of Reichenau, whose revision and completion of the astrolabe corpus, as well as his works on rhythmomachy, the abacus and music theory, became very popular.[38] Of all the cities in Lotharingia, Liège was the most important. It was called the Lotharingian Athens. Raoul was a student of the first *scolasticus* of

Liège cathedral, Wazo, and the second half of the eleventh century was dominated by the personality of another *scolasticus*, Franco, who held the position from 1047 to 1083. Liège was renowned for the study of music, and the popular *Geometry II* of Pseudo-Boethius, which included a section on the abacus with Hindu-Arabic numerals, appears to have been composed there.[39]

Knowledge of the abacus in England preceded the arrival of Lotharingian doctrine. For already in Harley MS 2506, the Abbo manuscript that contains the *Preceptum canonis Ptolomaei*, there is a brief abacus text.[40] There is no doubt, however, about the importance of the Lotharingian influence on English science. The earliest influence may have been indirect – through Bernelinus, if he was in Paris. But already before the Norman Conquest clerics had been invited to England directly from Lotharingia. One of these was Giso, bishop of Bath and Wells. Another was the Adelard whom King Harold invited to be *scolasticus* of the college of canons he founded at Waltham, to which we shall have reason to return. Lotharingian influence had even penetrated Wales before the end of the eleventh century, for Cotton MS Faustina C I, which begins with the only known copy of Rhygyfarch ap Sulien's lament on the destruction of his civilised and learned world by the Norman Conquest, contains part of the correspondence of Ragimbold and Raoul as a long gloss, alongside glosses in Welsh, to Macrobius's commentary on Cicero's *Dream of Scipio*.[41] Again it would be tempting to see the Lotharingians with their Arabic science as allies of the native Celts and Anglo-Saxons, against the Norman nobles who were usurping their lands, but this would be too simplistic a view. For the Norman kings continued to invite Lotharingians to take key ecclesiastical and administrative posts. The reason, before and after the Conquest, appears to have been pragmatic: secular schools had not yet developed in England, and the monks trained in the monasteries could not leave their monasteries to fulfil functions as bishops or royal servants.[42]

One important Lotharingian was Robert, bishop of Hereford. His Lotharingian origins are proved by several documents, and Julia Barrow has given strong reasons to believe that he was from Liège.[43] He may have arrived in England already before the

Conquest, if he is the same as Robert the clerk of Edward the Confessor, who first appears c. 1050. He was appointed bishop of Hereford in 1079, and held the see until his death in 1095. He modelled the episcopal chapel on that of Aachen, and introduced certain Liégeois customs in his reorganisation of the diocese. He brought into England the chronicle of Marianus Scotus (of Fulda and Mainz) and his commentary to it became an important computistic work.[44] William of Malmesbury describes his achievements in the abacus, the computus, and in investigating 'the course of the celestial stars'.[45] It is worth, however, pausing over another description of his mathematical prowess.

At Robert's death, Geoffrey, prior of Winchester, complained that Robert's '*mathesis* did not prolong his life, nor did the abacus which numbers the years in a different way.'[46] Additions on the abacus need no explanation (though there might also be a hint to the contrast between the infinite numbers that can be added on the abacus[47] and the finiteness of mortal life); 'mathesis', however, clearly refers to astrology in this context. As we have seen, the *Liber Alchandrei Philosophi* includes predictions of the length of life, and so does Firmicus Maternus's astrological textbook, which, significantly, has the title 'Mathesis'. We have another testimony to his involvement in astrology; for there is a story that, in 1091, Robert foretold from the stars that the dedication of Lincoln Cathedral, to which he had been invited, would not take place, and he saved himself the trouble of going.[48]

Another Lotharingian was Walcher, who became prior of Great Malvern, outside Worcester. He was using an astrolabe in 1109,[49] and was described at his death in 1135 as being a 'philosopher, astronomer, geometer and abacist'. We shall return to him.

★ ★ ★ ★ ★

Let us take stock of this scientific learning in England, whose sources, as I am suggesting, are on the one hand Orléans and Chartres, and on the other hand Lotharingia. It is based on the subjects of the quadrivium, each with their concomitant instruments: Boethius's *De arithmetica* and the game of rhythmomachy representing arithmetic, the *Geometria incerti auctoris* and the abacus representing geometry, Boethius's *De musica*, and the monochord representing music, and various texts on cosmology and the stars, and the astrolabe for astronomy. To the latter may be attached the Alchandrean corpus and Firmicus Maternus's *Mathesis*. In addition to instruments, mnemonic verse is used to facilitate the teaching of these subjects. The Arabic elements in this corpus are Hindu-Arabic numerals on the abacus, and possibly the abacus's imitation of pen-reckoning, the astrolabe (both the instrument and the texts describing its construction and use), and sections of the Alchandrean corpus. No knowledge of the Arabic language itself on the part of English scholars is betrayed so far.

A good example of a manuscript serving this curriculum is Royal MS 15. B. IX, which includes Hermann the Lame's collection of works on the astrolabe and the sundial, an astronomical instrument described by Gerbert d'Aurillac, and correspondence between Adelbold of Utrecht and Gerbert concerning the area of an equilateral triangle (see Plate 2, and Figs 7–10). Another example is Bodleian Library, Auct. F.1.9, the manuscript written in Worcester Cathedral Priory between 1120 and 1140 that we will frequently return to. This includes Bernelinus's treatise on the abacus, and the *De utilitatibus astrolabii*, as well as the earliest copy of the astronomical tables of al-Khwārizmī in the version of Adelard of Bath.

Adelard's father, Fastrad, might have come from Lotharingia, and was one of the wealthiest tenants of the Lotharingian bishop of Bath and Wells, Giso. Adelard himself, however, as he keeps reminding us, is a native of Bath. He went for his education to the cathedral schools of Laon and Tours. By the late eleventh century Laon had become an important cathedral school under the brothers Raoul and Anselm; Raoul was the author of an abacus text in the Gerbertian tradition.[50] Tours, in turn, had established a reputation as a centre of scholarship under bishop Berengar (d. 1088), who had been a student of Fulbert of Chartres. Adelard refers to a famous teacher there who explained to him the science of astronomy. Using some of the Latin

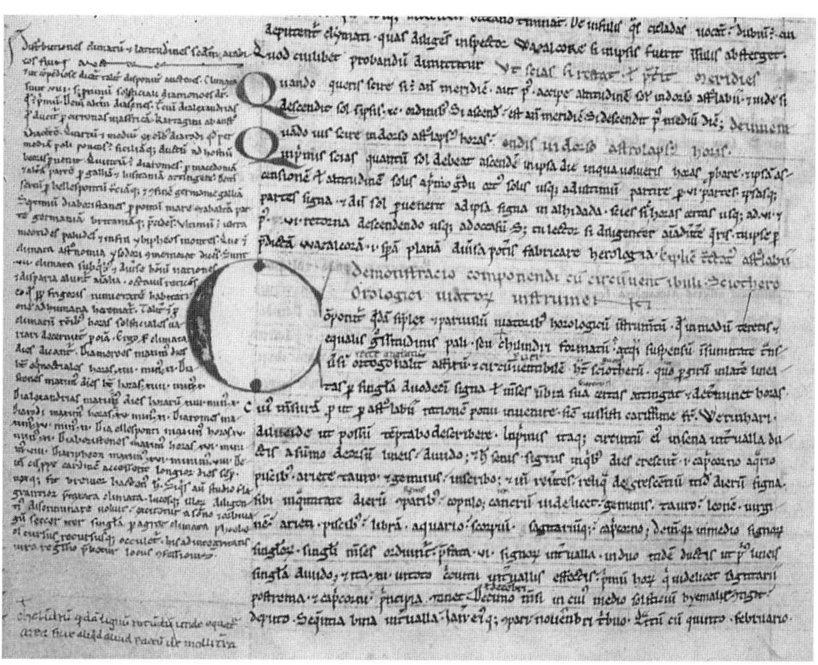

FIG.7. Royal MS 15.B.IX, fol.58v. A gloss at the end of *De utilitatibus astrolabii* contrasting the distribution of the climes according to the Arabs with the native Latin tradition of Isidore and Martianus Capella.

FIG.8. Royal MS 15.B.IX, fol.61r. The astrolabe chapters of the *Geometria incerti auctoris* (Bubnov, *Gerberti opera mathematica*, p.313). Note that a Latin word for the alidade – 'mediclinium' – has been glossed with the Arabic term: 'ahildada' (Arabic: *al-'iḍāda*), which (in several different spellings) soon became the standard term. The paragraphs instruct how to measure the heights of buildings in different circumstances, such as when there is a river in the way, and how to measure the breadth of a flat area.

De altitudine cum astrolabio metienda

Si fuerit altitudo in equalitate tali posite intuitui inspectione dimetiatur ab aliquo
astrolabium · et in medietate quadrati in ypothenusa et planicie erectum constituatur · me
diclinum · ut hac · s · positione stet · [r. altitudinis] mediclinum alterius partis astrolabii in numero graduum
[singularitatis · graduum] decem · xlv · et tam diu ab eo ante et retro estimando progrediatur · donec per utrumque ipsius mediclinum
[punctum] foramen altitudinis summitas inspiciatur · Et inspecta · loco in quo stetit mensor · nota inprimatur · et huic
inpressioni statura mensoris adiungatur · Post hoc locus ipse diligenter notetur · et ab eo usque ad radicem alti
tudinis tota planicies caute mensuretur · et quot pedum ipsa planicies fuerit · tot sine dubio altitu
do erit · Si vero non in medietate quadrati mediclinum steterit · sed in primo · aut secundo aut tercio aut in
aliquo quadrati gradu · xxx · graduum collatis qualis fuerit collatio ut illos quadrati gradus et xii · talis
erit inter planiciem et altitudinem mensurandam statura mensoris adiuncta · Ad altitudinem inaccessibilem cum ho[roscopo]

Ad altitudinem inaccessibilem ob fluminis vel vallis impedimentum · Sit altitudo quelibet [horoscopo metienda]
ut est · a · d · Sitque fluminis vel vallis impedimentum ut est · b · c · Sume [vel astrolabium] horoscopum stans in ripa · c · et per utrumque
foramen mediclinum summitatem · a · diligenter inspice · Considera numerum graduum in mense quadrato · quem ubi causa
notetur quaternario numero per quem summa totius quadrati · scilicet · xlviii · dividatur · et quarta pars ex parte indiviso
[duodecim · iii · singularis · xlviii ·]
contribuatur · Post hoc de · c · ad · d · certa spacii quantitas metiatur · que exempli gratia · xl · pedum proponatur · Iterum sume
horoscopum stans in fine · d · et per utrumque foramen ut prius summitatem · a · inspice perpende iterum numerum graduum in
quadrato quem signaturum tuarum numero per quem demum summa totius quadrati dividatur · et pars tercia que est
xlviii · iuxta certa quod est · xvi · contribuatur · et minor numerus de maiore · id est · xxx · de xlviii · tollatur · et quod rema
net · id est · xii · cum latere quadrati quod est · xii · comparetur · Minimus remanens · et latus quadrati equalis pronuncietur ·
Et sic minimum remanens · in quadrati lateri · iii · equale habetur · sic spacium · d · c · spacio · a · b · equale affir
metur · Et quota pars minimi quis est utrumque numerus graduum · in · iii · indicetur · eadem pars · a · b · spacium · d · b ·
spacio sine dubio dicatur · Exempli gratia · xl · a · b · sic est · xl · c · d · et est · clx · totum · b · d · et est · cxx · b · c · Item de eodem cum

Si quid eminens inaccessibile fuerit estimandum cum horoscopo · Stet alta mensor [horoscopo]
in metiendi eminencias altissimo · Suscipiatque per utrumque mediclinum foramen · quousque intueatur alti
tudinis mensurande acumen · Et inspecto · gradus quadrati numerentur · quod exempli manifestacione in
venitur · quod in · xii · quadrati latere quater continetur · Hic per · viii · tam diu ab eo ante et retro progrediatur · donec iam visum cacumen
altitudinis metiende tamen videatur · Et viso numerus graduum quadrati demum inspiciatur · et ubi gratia · vi · habe
antur · quia in · xii · in quadrati latere secies continetur non dubitatur · et intervallum stacionum mensoris · in pedum no
tabile habetur · his peractis · numerus continens ternarium · de ternario de maiori continetur · id est senario semel tollatur
et binarius qui remanet unitate habetur · et ipsum intervallum stacionum mensoris duplum in
accessibilis alti dicatur · Sic ut quod dictum in omnibus notum habetur · uni
versalis in nullo vacillans ponatur · Subtractione continentium minoris
facta · si unum remanserit · intervallum stacionum mensoris · alto equale erit
si vero · ii · duplum · si · iii · triplum · et sic in sequentibus · Tali pictura fit declaratio
picta ad altitudinem cum horoscopo metiendam ·

Si vis cum horoscopo quamlibet metiri planiciem · dirige intuitum per utrumque
foramen mediclinum · donec terminum eius intuitus in metiende quantitatis limite · Post hoc in quo gradu quadrati medi
clinum stet inspiciatur · Et ipse numerus graduum superior cum · iii · conferatur · et quota proporcio fuerit graduum ad · iii · tali
proporcione stature metientis ad totam planiciem · Verbi gratia · Sit statura mensoris · a · b · planicies · b · c · numerus graduum
· iii · quod ad · iii · comparatur · quota pars eius dubitatione sublata inveniatur · Et · a · b · que est statura metientis sic · b · c · in
planicie quota pars invenietur · Sic ternarii in · iii · pars · iiii · comparatur ·

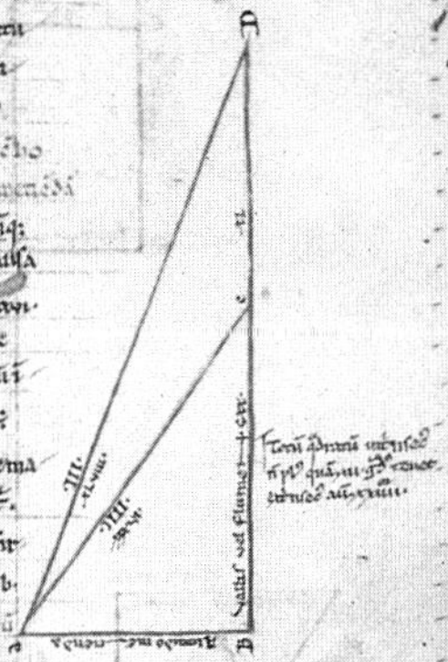

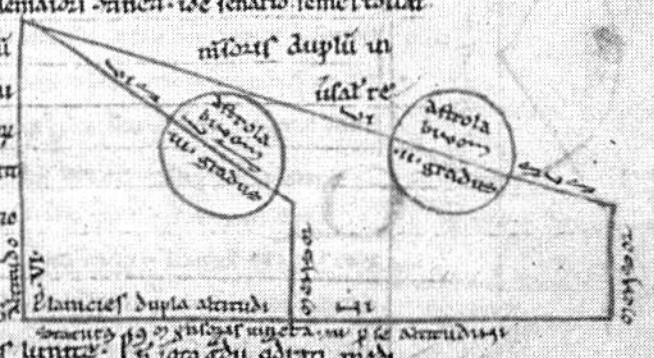

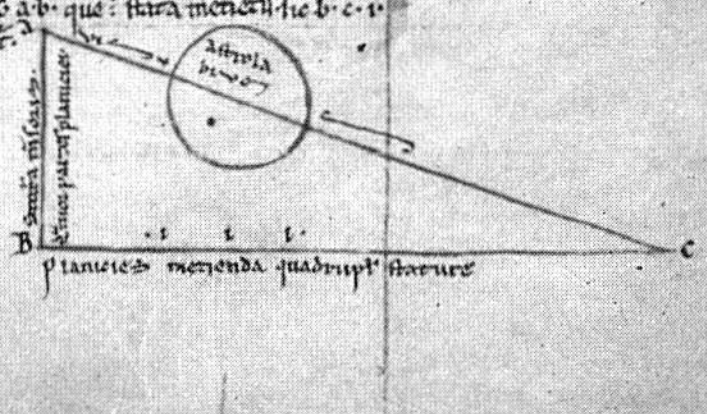

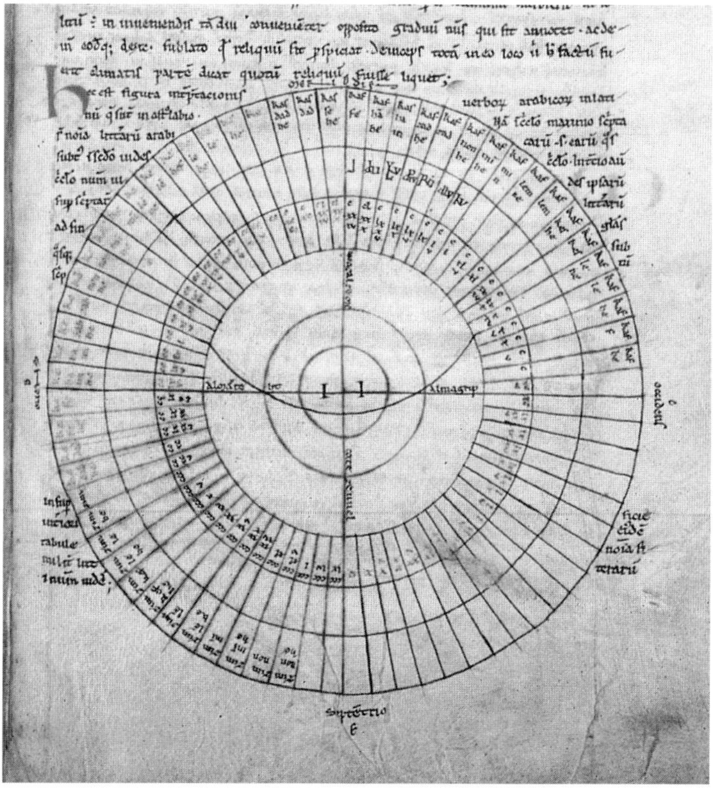

FIG.9 Royal MS 15.B.IX, fol.71r. A chapter on the interpretation of Arabic names of numbers (the 'abjad' system; ed. Bubnov, *Gerberti opera mathematica*, p.146), on an astrolabe plate, which causes the scribe some problems. In the middle band the scribe attempts to write Arabic letters for numbers, and soon gives up. He perseveres for longer in writing them in transliteration in the outer band. In the centre of the diagram there are further Arabic words, with further corruptions: 'almagrip' for *al-maghrib* = the west; 'alma\z/reht' for *al-mashriq* = the east; 'cate zeuuel' for *al-khaṭṭ al-zawāl* and 'wazalzeme' for *wasaṭ as-samā'* for the northern and southern extensions of the meridian line; see Kunitzsch, *Glossar der arabischen Fachausdrücke in der mittelalterlichen europäischen Astrolabliteratur*, Göttingen, 1983, nos. 24, 27, 14 and 57.

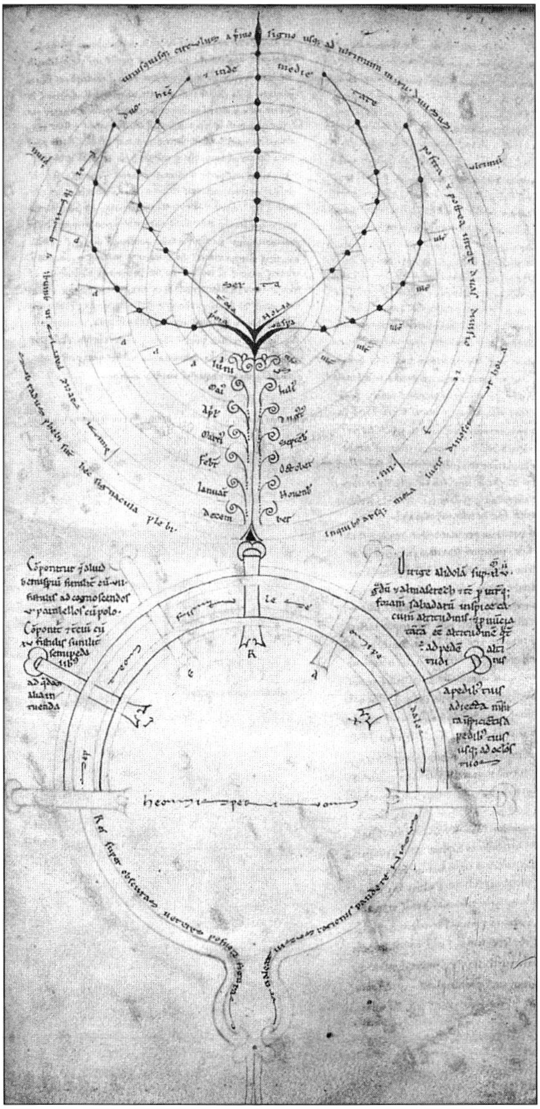

FIG.10 Royal MS 15.B.IX, fol.77r. The upper image is of a sundial, with the verses:

Sub radiis Phebi
sunt hec signacula plebi
in quibus absque mora
lucis dinoscitur hora.

The lower image is of the hemisphere described by Gerbert d'Aurillac for his friend Constantine of Micy (ed. Bubnov, *Gerberti opera mathematica*, pp.24–8). Once again there are verses, on the diagram itself:

Septem fistule semipedales
res super obscuras
veteres posuere figuras
ut valeat visus
rationis pandere nisus.

sources already mentioned, he wrote his own text on the abacus,[51] and his introduction to the seven liberal arts – the *De eodem et diverso*. The latter work shows direct knowledge of Boethius's arithmetic and music and the *Geometria incerti auctoris*, and refers to the use of the abacus. In the tradition of Fulbert, a poem accompanies Adelard's text on the abacus, to facilitate remembering the strange names for the counters:[52]

De caracteribus abaci

1 Ordine primogeno iam nomen possidet ygin.
2 Andras ecce locum mox vendicat ipse secundum.
3 Ormis post numeros incompositus sibi primus.
4 Denique bis binos succedens indicat arbas.
5 Significat quinque ficto de nomine quimas.
6 Exa tenet calctis perfecto munere gaudens.
7 Zenis enim digne septeno fulget honore.
8 Octo beatificos themenias exprimit unus,
9 Terque notat trinum selentis[53] nomine rithmum.
10 Hinc sequitur sipos;[54] est qui rota nempe vocatus.[55]

The symbols of the abacus

1 Of the first-born in order *Ygin* now possesses the title.
2 Behold, *Andras* soon claims the next place himself.
3 After these numbers *Ormis* is the first to be incomposite in itself.
4 Finally *Arbas* in the next place indicates two twos.
5 *Quimas* with its invented name signifies five.
6 *Calctis* holds six, enjoying a perfect gift.
7 For *Zenis* worthily shines with the seventh honour.
8 One *Themenias* expresses the blessed eight.
9 *Selentis* notes by its name the thrice-three measure.
10 Here follows *Sipos* which is also called, of course, the 'wheel'.[56]

After his formal training in the Latin schools Adelard embarked on a journey which took him to Magna Graecia and the Principality of Antioch. It is this seven-year journey which he describes, famously, as his quest for the *studia Arabum* ('the studies of the Arabs'), which he contrasts to the *Gallica studia* ('French studies'). These are studies based on reason rather than authority. But the result of these studies is not, this time, the mathematics and astronomy promoted by Maslama and his school in Córdoba or the abacus with *apices*. It is, rather, the work on natural science and medicine, which was the interest of scholars in Salerno and Montecassino. It is in these two places that Constantine the African had been translating medical works from Arabic into Latin. Constantine was in Salerno by 1077 and in Monte Cassino before 1087, and had died before 1098/9. His principal work was an adaptation for a Latin audience of the *Kitāb Kāmil aṣ-ṣinā'a aṭ-ṭibbīya* ('the complete' – or 'perfect' – 'book of the medical art') of 'Alī ibn al-'Abbās al-Majūsī (writing before 977/8). This work Constantine called the *Pantegni*. It consisted of ten books of theory of medicine and an equal number on practical medicine, and aside from being the most comprehensive book on medicine of its time was also important for dealing with elementary physics.[57] Constantine translated several other works – on diets, the stomach, melancholy, forgetfulness and sexual intercourse – by doctors in Qayrawan (in present-day Tunisia), the Zīrid capital, from where he himself had originated.

Although there is nothing chronologically against the supposition that Adelard would have got to know these translations when he visited Magna Graecia, he makes no mention of Constantine, and the medical discussions in his *Natural Questions* are never verbal quotations from Constantine's translations. In fact, it is quite clear that Adelard is following a genre which was actively pursued in Magna Graecia from before the time of the translation-activity of Constantine and his school. Adelard's *De eodem et diverso* and *Natural Questions* must be regarded as close to each other in date, and both reflecting (in respect to their scientific knowledge) the predominantly *Greek* learning of Salerno in the early years of the twelfth century. This source is clearly stated in the *De eodem et diverso*, in which Adelard says that, passing through Magna Graecia on the way from Salerno, he 'put to the test with his opinions a certain Greek philosopher who, more than anything else, could talk about the art of medicine and the natures of things'.[58] And Greek learning is appropriate for a work dedicated to a bishop of Syracuse, a Greek-speaking part of Sicily. Although the *Natural Questions* purport to give the

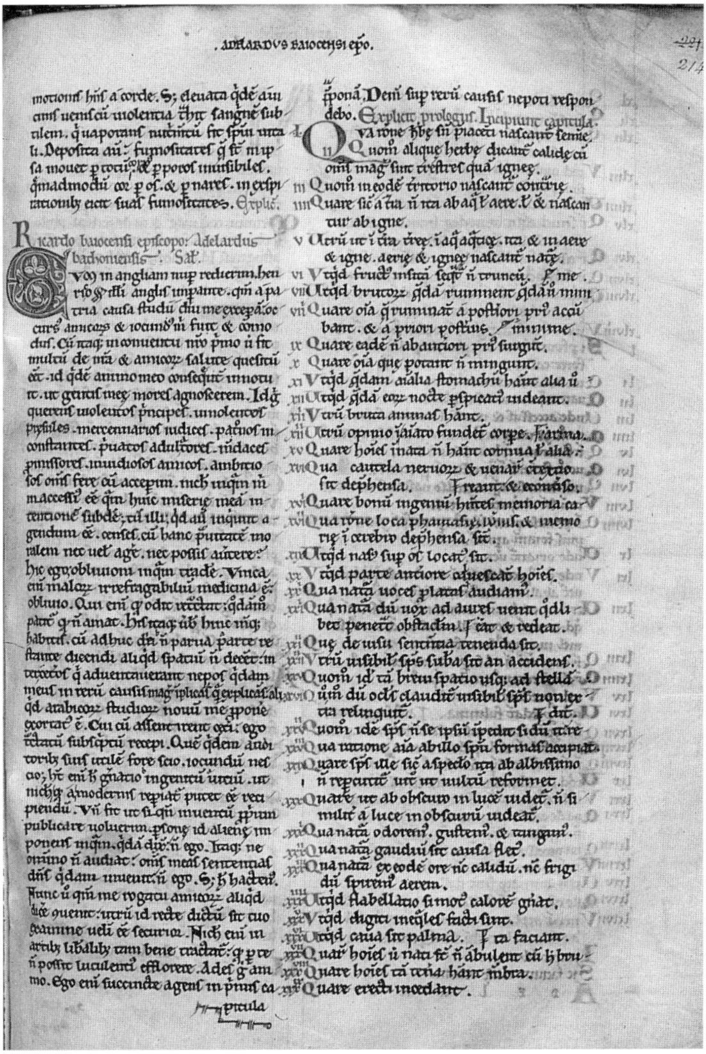

FIG.11. Cotton MS Galba E.IV, fol.214r. The opening of Adelard's *Natural Questions*. Note the reference to 'arabicorum studiorum' in the 17th line from the bottom of the first column.

result of Adelard's *studia Arabum*, their sources are remarkably close to the works by Alfano, archbishop of Salerno (1058–85). These include Nemesius's *On the nature of man*, a work with limited circulation, which was translated from Greek by Alfano, and it is tempting to think that Adelard's *Natural Questions* might somehow be related to the now lost 'Alfani Salernitanensis de quibusdam questionibus medicinalibus' that was once in the library of Christchurch Cathedral Priory, Canterbury.[59]

One indication of this predominantly Greek Salernitan learning in England is the earliest collection of texts that include Adelard's *Natural Questions*. This is Cotton MS, Galba E. IV, written in the mid-twelfth century and belonging to the Benedictine Abbey of Bury St Edmunds (Fig. 11). The Salernitan works in this manuscript include Alfano's translation of Nemesius, another version of the chapter on the elements in Nemesius's work, and a substantial text on the elements by Marius Salernitanus,[60] as well as works by (Pseudo-)Galen and Soranus. There are no translations from Arabic here, but the manuscript does witness to the fact that the communication lines between England and Salerno were wide open.

But one cannot separate the Greek and Arabic learning of Salerno and South Italy very sharply. In fact, the earliest manuscript in England of one of Constantine's Arabic translations could also be found at Bury St Edmunds. This manuscript is now Wellcome 801A, a manuscript of the medical collection known later as the *Articella*, which included Constantine's translation of the 'Questions on medicine' by Ḥunayn b. Isḥāq (the '*Isagoge* of Johannitius'). The manuscript is written in the Beneventan script of Southern Italy in the early to mid-twelfth century.[61] Bury St Edmunds also possessed at least two manuscripts of Constantine's *Pantegni*, one of which survives in the library of Trinity College, Cambridge.[62] The same translation of Nemesius's chapter on the elements as that found in Cotton MS Galba E.IV recurs in only one other manuscript (as far as we know), and that is a *Pantegni* manuscript in the British Library, Add. MS 22719 (Fig. 12). This manuscript belonged to the priory of St Nicholas in Exeter, a cell of Battle Abbey.[63]

The theoretical books of the *Pantegni* are followed by the

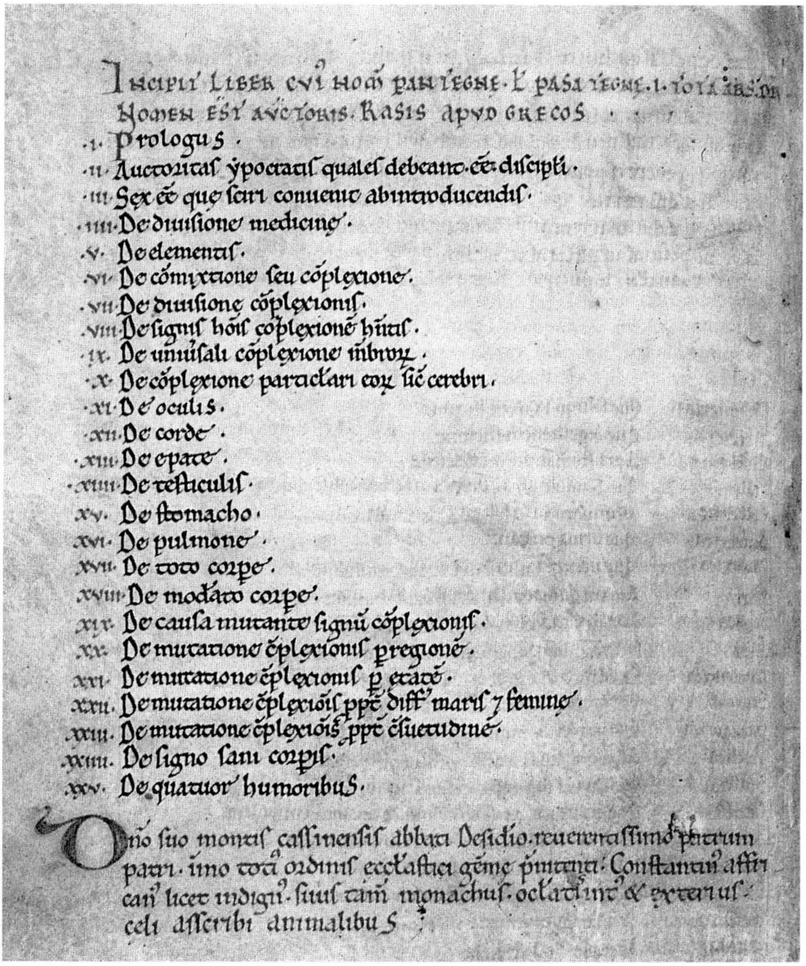

FIG. 12. Add. MS 22719, fol. 2v. The title-page of Constantine's *Pantegni*. Note that here the *Pantegni* is attributed to 'Rasis', the renowned Arabic doctor Abū Bakr Muḥammad ibn Zakarīyā' ar-Rāzī, to whom the *Pantegni* is attributed in several early manuscripts of the text; see C. Burnett, 'Encounters with Rāzī the Philosopher: Constantine the African, Petrus Alfonsi and Ramón Martí', in *Pensamiento hispano medieval: homenaje a Horatio Santiago-Otero*, Madrid, 1997, (in press).

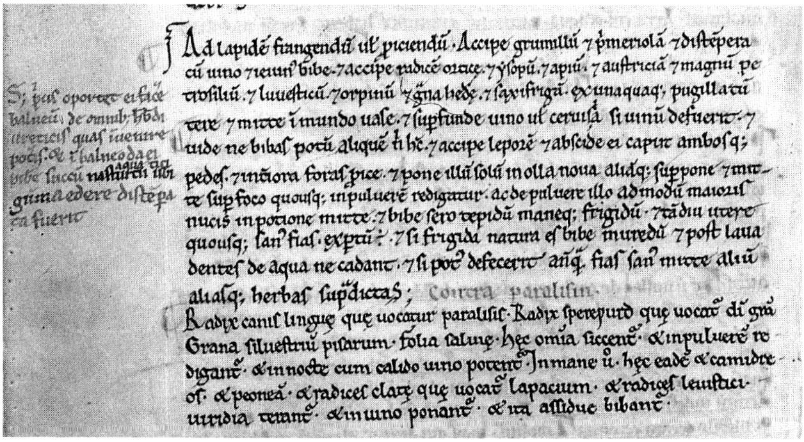

FIG. 13. Add. MS 22719, fol. 163v. Recipes of English provenance. Note the phrases 'For paralysis: the root of a dog's tongue, which is called "paralisis". The root of "spearwort" which is called "the grace of God"'.

chapter on the elements from Nemesius, after which a page has been filled up with recipes including English words (Fig. 13). Then come the practical books of the *Pantegni*, which in turn are followed by the earliest surviving copy of a curious work examining the validity of using magical remedies, written originally in Arabic by Qusṭā ibn Lūqā.[64] Qusṭā asks whether magical recipes – such as the right foot of a tortoise hung from the affected limb, as a cure for gout – have any effect, and, if so, why? His conclusion is that they are effective, and this is because of the powers of suggestion. This work has thus been considered to be an early example of the justification of the placebo effect.[65]

In this copy the text has neither title nor author. It is assumed that it was translated by Constantine, because of its juxtaposition to the *Pantegni* in this manuscript and its attribution to Constantine by Roger Bacon.[66] But this early copy already betrays a British element in the transmission of the text. For, Scotland is mentioned as an example of a cold country (Fig. 14). It is hardly likely that either Qusṭā ibn Lūqā or Constantine

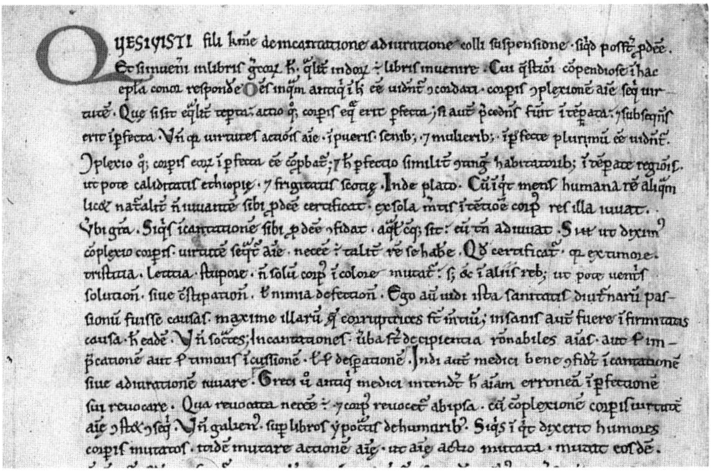

FIG.14. Add. MS 22719, fol.200v. The beginning of Qusṭā ibn Lūqā's *De phisicis ligaturis*. Note the reference to Scotland ('Scotię') in the seventh line of the text.

would have written this; with Constantine's classicising tendencies it is much more probable that he would have been referring to the land of the Hyperborean Scythians: 'Scytiae'. Is 'Scotiae' a conscious (or subconscious) change on the part of a British scribe?

One puzzling fact concerning the Salernitan material of which I have been giving examples is that the English manuscripts are as early, if not earlier, than manuscripts in Italy or elsewhere, and that works supposedly written by Salernitan masters include English words.[67] One can only suppose that the contacts between England and South Italy were very close, and this supposition is substantiated by the presence of several doctors from Salerno in England, or Englishmen who went to study in Salerno.[68]

One of these Englishmen was Adelard, as witnessed not only by his own testimony, but also by the presence of his *Natural Questions* in a manuscript of Salernitan material, as we have seen.

The manuscript which gives the most authoritative text of the *Natural Questions*, however, points in another direction. This manuscript is now broken up into three parts, shared between the University Library of Leiden and the Bibliothèque nationale in Paris.[69] It is the only manuscript to include Adelard's *De eodem et diverso* as well. It also contains an excerpt from the *Pantegni* (on the soul), and a version of Pseudo-Quintilian's *Declamationes maiores* in dialogue form.

Now, the only reference in a medieval catalogue to the presence of the *De eodem et diverso* is in the late twelfth-century catalogue of Waltham Abbey (Fig. 15). This catalogue lists Adelard's two works in the same order as they occur in the Leiden-Paris manuscript, as well as a version of Pseudo-Quintilian's *Declamationes maiores*, which it attributes to Adelard.[70] The text in the Leiden-Paris manuscript is unique in having two authorial additions: it was apparently Adelard's final word on *Natural Questions*. There is a strong likelihood that it was copied from manuscripts in Waltham Abbey, and therefore witnesses a privileged position for Adelard's works in the library there. Is it a mere coincidence that, as we have seen, the *scolasticus* of the college of canons founded by Harold Godwinson in Waltham was also called Adelard, and came from Lotharingia? That Giso, bishop of Bath and Wells, whose tenant Adelard of Bath's father was, was the only English bishop to attend the consecration of the Abbey? That Waltham Abbey possessed not only several of Constantine the African's translations and a copy of the *Articella*, but also the older works on the computus and the abacus? That King Harold made lavish donations to the Abbey (which was destined to become the resting place of his body), and that William the Conqueror got into trouble for stealing some precious books from its library?[71] Perhaps there is some truth after all that Adelard of Bath used the 'books of king Harold', at least in his early writings on hawking and the abacus. For his direct translations from Arabic, as we shall see in the next lecture, he would have used a very different source.

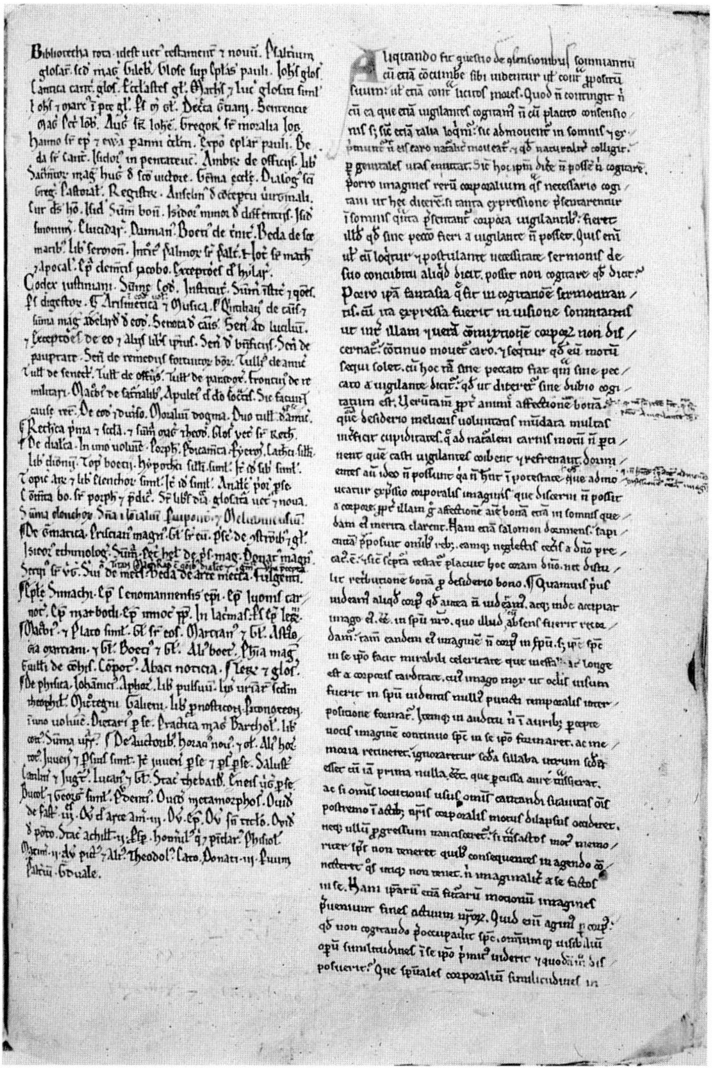

FIG. 15. Waltham Abbey Bible (Passmore Edwards Museum), fol. 156r. Catalogue of the library, including three works by Adelard of Bath.

PLATE 1. Harley MS 3487, fol.202r. The beginning of Qusṭā ibn Lūqā's *On the difference between the spirit and the soul.* The subject-matter has inspired an illustration which introduces religious elements not in the text itself: God is above, blessing with his right hand and holding a book in his left. Two naked human beings issue from the mouth of the dead person; presumably they are the 'natural' and the 'animal spirit' which, according to Qusṭā, leave the dead body through the mouth; see ed. Wilcox, lines 50–54: 'Eius [*scil.* spiritus] quoque exitus fit ex ore tempore motus oris quando scilicet apperitur os et non potest amplius a se claudi, sed iam necesse est ut claudatur propter annullationem vite post ab eo separat spiritum'. In a marginal sketch for this illumination the dying man is portrayed naked.

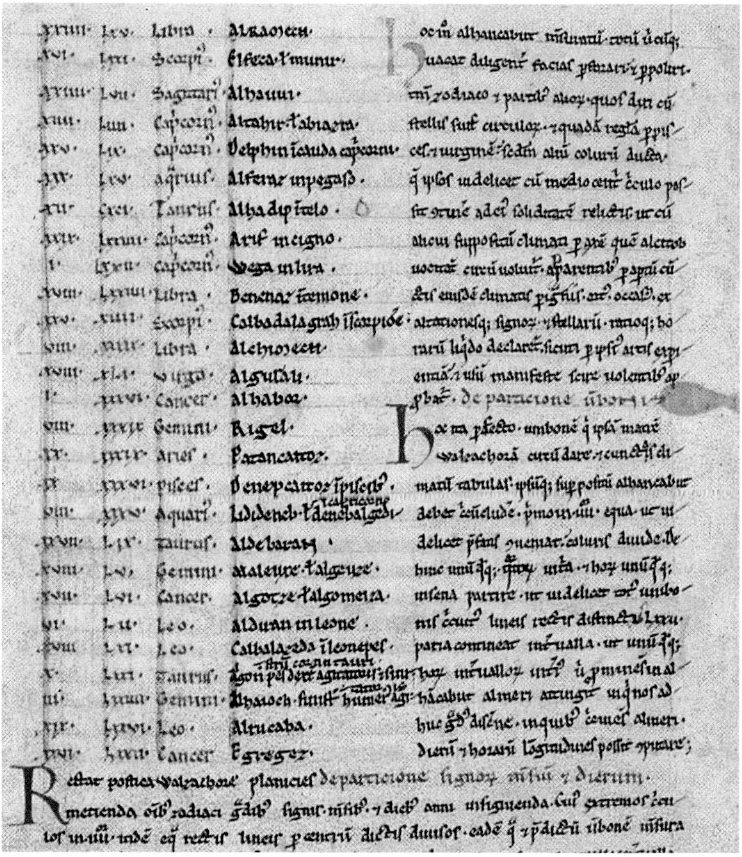

PLATE 2. Royal MS 15.B.IX, fol.52v. Important stars on the rete of the astrolabe (= *De mensura astrolabii* h''). They all have Arabic names: 'alramech, Elfeca vel munir, alhauui, altahir' , i.e., *al-rāmiḥ, al-munīr min al-fakka, ra's al-ḥawwā'* and *al-nasr al-ṭā'ir*, see P. Kunitzsch, *Typen von Sternverzeichnissen in astronomischen Handschriften des 10.–14. Jh.*, Wiesbaden, 1966, s.v.

PLATE 3. Oxford, Bodleian Library, Auct. F.1.9, fol.99v. The beginning of Adelard of Bath's version of the tables of al-Khwārizmī. The Arabic terms and the numerals are written in red.

Incipit ezich elkauerezmi

INCIPIT EZICH ELKAUREZMI PER ADELARDUM BATHONIENSEM EX ARABICO SUMPTUS.

LIBER iste septem planetarum atque draconis statum continet a medio mercurii die usque ad medium diem iouis determinatum. Secundum hoc etiam et in ceteris feriis idem conuenit, a medio die scilicet precedentis usque ad sequentis medium. Quoniam autem medius dies mercurii initium fuit elhigere et elmuharram, ideo ab eo et ezich sumpsit initium. Posita itaque in hoc uolumine ab elkaurezmo est examinatio planetarum et temporum secundum medium locum terre ARIN, a quo quidem in quattuor mundi terminos equalis habetur distantia .xc. uidelicet gradus secundum quartam circuli partem. Quoniam enim omnes terre regiones describere omniaque tempora determinare et tediosum et inexplicabile pro temporibus innumeris meridies primis infimas centrum terre annotata sunt, eo scilicet tenore ut ab hac radice per regulas geometricales et arithmeticas ceteras regiones et tempora determinare non difficile sit. Interim itaque id a lectore postulatum sit, ut si harum artium immunis accesserit, quicquid in his computationum lineis secundum regulas subscriptas inciderit, magis certum quam necessarium habeat. Cum uero et eis imbutus fuerit et elizmg congestionem et ptolomei attemptauerit, omnia que hic procedunt necessario peruenire non dubitabit. Hactenus hec. Nunc uero quoniam hic temporum transitus cum planetarum cursu comparatur, de eis primo agendum est.

DE TERMINO ANNI ARABUM.

ANNUS igitur arabum secundum lune cursum consideratur. Id enim tempus annum uocant quod luna a solis coniunctione discedens duodecies eum attingendo metitur, quod .ccc.l.iiii. diebus continetur cum additione .v.te et .vi.te partis diei. Est autem quinta et sexta diei partes .xi.cim quarum .xxx. in die. Si enim dies in .xxx.ta diuidatur partes, erunt earum .xi.cim toti diei quinta et sexta. He additiones dum medietas diei aut ea minus fuerint non computantur, eritque annus .ccc.lv. dierum. Cum uero medietate maius explebitur, dies integer computabitur, eritque annus .ccc.lv. dierum, dicitque hic annus lingua arabica elkebicee. Est itaque annus arabum hic .xii.cim inse menses continens, quorum primus quidem almuharram dierum .xxx. Secundus uero azafar dierum .xxviiii. sicque de ceteris uariatim, ut subscripta demonstrat tabula, excepto eo quod ultimus quidem dulheia cum sua positione .xxv. uel .iiii. dierum sit. Ex supradictis partibus creato die ipse etiam .xxx. dierum quandoque supputatur. Ex his itaque id accidit ut initium anni arabum, id est elmuharram, uariato transitu quandoque in hieme quandoque in estate accidit.

DE TERMINO ANNI ROMANORUM.

ANNI autem romanorum secundum cursum solis diebus .ccc. et .lx.v. et quarta diei parte continetur. Hec autem additio dum quarta uel media fuerit non computabitur; cum autem medietate diei maior dies integer ponetur, eritque annus .ccc.lxvi. dierum, dicitque a romanis bissextalis. Continet autem annus romanus menses .xii. quorum primus october .xxx. et unum diem habens, nouember uero .xxx., december .xxxi. et quartam ponitur, quia bissextus in fine decembris. Unde idem mensis annis tribus .xxx. et .i. dierum, quarto uero .xxx. et duorum computabitur. Ianuarius uero .xxxi.mus, februarius .xx. et .viii., martius .xxxi., aprilis .xxx., maius .xxxi., iunius .xxx., iulius .xxxi., augustus .xxxi., september .xxx. Secundum hanc igitur anni positionem palam est quod annus romanorum qui et alexandri dicitur anno arabum diebus .xi.cim maior reperitur. Si quis uero numero supradictorum annorum crescente scire uelit quot anni arabici a quot annis romanis parte contineantur, et hos et illos dies dissoluat, sicque palam erit eorum conuenientia. Quoniam itaque liber iste diuersis nationibus prodesse potest, quarum non omnes idem tempus obseruant, ideo sequens pagina tempora tam diuersorum regum quam prouinciarum continens subscripta est, ut cum precepta hec secundum tempus elhigere regni alexandri et annos arabum data et notata sunt, tam et tempus illud et anni ipsi in quaslibet aliarum nationum reduci possint.

DE NUMERORUM PRESCRIPTIONIBUS.

HIS hactenus explicatis hoc etiam addendum est, ut quoniam fere omnes huius libri pagine nomine mensium uel annorum planorum uel annorum arabicorum prętitulate sunt, quod sibi uelit hec prosignatio intimetur. Considerantes itaque phylosophi planetarum totas rotarum deinde circumferentias rotasque in signa, signa in gradus, gradus in dakaicas, dakaicas in secundas diuidentes, quarum istarum partium

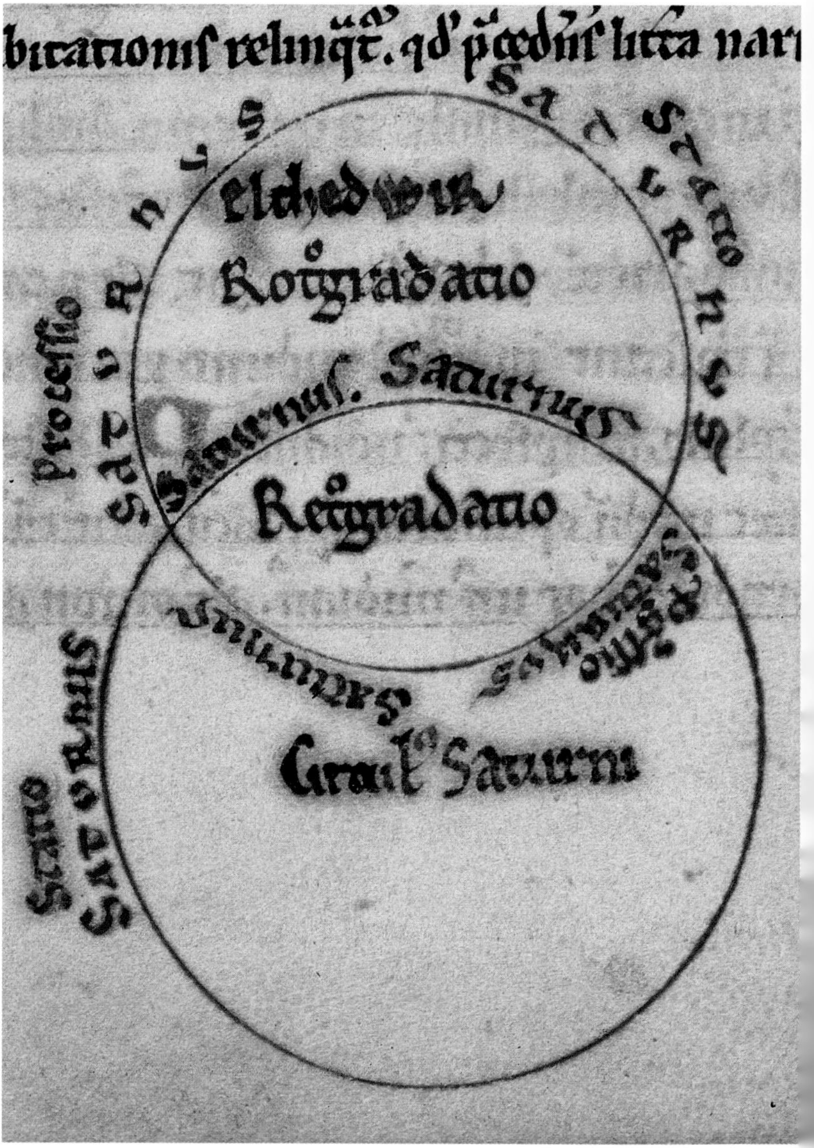

PLATE 4. Arundel MS 377, fol.101v. The movement of Saturn, illustrating Daniel of Morley's *Philosophia.* The course of Saturn on an epicycle ('elthedwir' – i.e., Arabic *al-tadwīr*) mounted on a circle ('circulus Saturni') whose centre is eccentric to the centre of the earth. Saturn's movement around an epicycle explains its apparent variation between going forward, stopping and going backwards, indicated here (rather approximately) by the terms 'processio', 'statio' and 'retrogradatio'. Compare the illustration and accompanying text in Adelard's *De opere astrolapsus*, MS Fitzwilliam Museum, McClean 165, fol.82r and ed. Dickey, pp.160–1.

The Education of Henry II

ADELARD OF BATH, at the beginning of his original work on the cosmos and the astrolabe (*De opere astrolapsus*), addressed Duke Henry, the future king Henry II, with the following words. The date is early in 1150 AD:

> I thoroughly approve of the fact that the nobility of a royal race applies itself to the study of the liberal arts. But I find it all the more remarkable that preoccupation in the affairs of government does not distract the mind from that study. Thus I understand that you, Henry, since you are the grandson of a king, have understood with the complete attention of your mind, what is said by Philosophy: that states are blest either if they are handed over for philosophers to rule, or if their rulers adhere to philosophy. Since your childhood was once imbued with the scent of this reasoning, your mind preserves it for a long time, and the more heavily it is weighed down by outside occupations, the more diligently it withdraws itself from them. Hence it happens that you not only read carefully and with understanding those things that the writings of the Latins contain, but you also dare to wish to understand the opinions of the Arabs concerning the sphere, and the circles and movements of the planets. For you say that whoever lives in a house, if he is ignorant of its material or composition, its size or kind, its position or parts, is not worthy of such a dwelling. Thus, whoever has been born

and brought up in the hall of the world, if he does not bother to get to know the reason behind such wonderful beauty after the age of discretion, is unworthy of that hall and, if it were possible, should be thrown out. Having been asked by you frequently to do this, although I am not confident in my own strength, nevertheless, so that I may join philosophy to nobility in an example from our own age, I will attempt to fulfil your demand as far as I am able. Therefore I shall write in Latin what I have learnt in Arabic about the world and its parts.[72]

There are several things to notice about this dedication: its emphasis on the qualities of the good ruler, its reference to Henry's reaching the age of discretion, and to his being the grandson of a king (i.e., Henry I). These indicate beyond doubt that Adelard is dedicating his work to Henry to celebrate a very important occasion: his investiture with the Dukedom of Normandy at the time of his coming of age. This happened on his return from England to Normandy either at the end of 1149, or more probably early in 1150. The specialness of the occasion is well brought out by the author of *Gesta Stephani*, who writes:

[On returning to Normandy Henry], welcomed magnificently by all who flocked together from every quarter on hearing of his arrival, was most amply honoured by everyone in the whole duchy as their lord and presented most lavishly with gifts.[73]

Adelard, too, contributed an appropriate gift. By this time he must have been quite an old man, and already had a reputation as a philosopher, and purveyor of Arabic wisdom – a reputation which had been spread by his books and his pupils.[74] His dedication suggests that Duke Henry already had some acquaintance with the *studia Arabum* and possibly with Adelard himself. Let us explore this further.

We know that Henry, who was born in 1133, was first put to school with Peter of Saintes, whom his father, Geoffrey Plantagenet, Count of Anjou, had chosen for him because he was 'more learned in poetry than anyone this side of the Pyrenees'.[75] He composed an erudite Latin poem on the story of Troy, and must have taught Henry the basics of grammar and good Latin. In 1142–4 Henry was with his mother, the Empress Matilda, in the Bristol house of his uncle Robert of Gloucester. Here he was taught 'letters and manners' by a certain 'Master Matthew'. After 1144 he was back on the Continent and did not return to England except for short periods in 1147 and in 1149–50.[76] It was during this period that William of Conches addressed his *Dragmaticon* to Geoffrey, who, in 1144, had become Duke of Normandy in addition to Count of Anjou. The tone of the dedication and certain phrases in the text,[77] suggest very strongly that Geoffrey had invited William to his court to teach his sons, the oldest of whom was Henry.[78]

William was returning to his native Normandy after a successful teaching career in Chartres and Paris, in which he followed the new method of teaching the secular arts inaugurated by the almost legendary Bernard of Chartres. Bernard's teaching was based on the *auctores*, the masterpieces of pagan Classical Latin that were on the curriculum because they taught the student how to write good Latin prose and poetry, but which, under Bernard and his students, became a vehicle for working out the functions of the universe and of man – i.e., for investigating natural philosophy, which otherwise had no place in the curriculum of the seven arts.[79] The *Dragmaticon* is William's masterpiece of natural philosophy, in which he brings to their most highly-developed form ideas that he had been nourishing in his earlier *Philosophia*, and his commentaries to Boethius's *Consolation of Philosophy* and Plato's *Timaeus*. The *Dragmaticon* owes its name to the fact that it is set out as a dramatic dialogue between the Duke of Normandy and his 'philosopher', William, presumably acted out in front of his docile sons. For William writes in the preface that 'I have proposed to write something pertaining to *scientia* for you and your *sons*.'[80]

The preceding phrase in the preface quotes the same metaphor from Horace about newly baked pots preserving the scent of their contents for a long time, as does Adelard in the above-quoted preface to his work *De opere astrolapsus*: 'The hope of the future lies in you and your sons; for, unlike other fathers, you have imbued them from a tender age not in games of dice, but in the study of letters, whose scent they will preserve for a long time, according to that statement of Horace: "By which it is once imbued etc." '[81] This parallel between the two works may not be coincidental. For the *Dragmaticon* and the *De opere astrolapsus* accompany each other in the manuscripts, as we shall see; and William also makes extensive use of Adelard's *Natural Questions*, which, as was mentioned in the first lecture, purported to convey the *studia Arabum* that Adelard had been investigating on a seven-year research trip which took in Southern Italy, Sicily and the Principality of Antioch.

Twenty years earlier, when writing his *Philosophia* in the 1120s, William already seems to have known Adelard's work, and to have been the first to know it.[82] This was probably in Chartres, where Adelard's version of the astronomical tables of al-Khwārizmī had already arrived by the early 1140s when Thierry of Chartres incorporated them into his collection of texts on the liberal arts: the *Heptateuchon*. Several English students were at Chartres during the bishoprics of Ivo (1090–1115/6) and Gaufrid de Lèves (until 1149).[83] William of Conches must have brought some of the learning of Chartres to the court of Geoffrey of Anjou, and that may have included the *Natural Questions*.

The use of the *Natural Questions* in the *Dragmaticon*, however, is more conspicuous and more extensive than that in the *Philosophia*,[84] and a more direct route for their arrival in the Norman court lay open. For Adelard had dedicated the work to Richard, bishop of Bayeux (necessarily the first of the two bishop Richards: Richard FitzSamson 1107–33), and a copy of the dedication manuscript was in the hands of bishop Richard's successor but one – Philip of Harcourt, bishop from 1142–63. It was given by him to the abbey of Bec, and another manuscript from Bec, which was very probably his – Avranches 235 – once contained two further texts by Adelard.[85] Thus we see an early penetration of Adelard's works into Normandy.

William of Conches clearly copied from Adelard rather than *vice versa*, for, to Adelard's doctrines he adds those from two sources not used by Adelard: the *Pantegni* of Constantine the African, which, as pointed out in the first lecture, was the first comprehensive compendium of medicine translated from Arabic into Latin, and Seneca's *Natural Questions*, whose earliest manuscripts were, significantly, written in Northern France in the twelfth century. In one group of manuscripts of that century, the *Natural Questions* of Adelard and Seneca are copied together.[86] Philip of Harcourt's manuscript of Adelard's *Natural Questions* was one such manuscript,[87] and William probably already knew the combination, if he was not himself responsible for it.

Thus, by early 1150, Duke Henry had received, in the company of his father, William of Conches's *Dragmaticon* which may have whetted his appetite for the *studia Arabum* of Adelard, and the dedication copy of *De opere astrolapsus* of Adelard himself, in which Adelard states that Henry had asked for the opinions of the Arabs. How closely Adelard was associated with Duke Henry's education is difficult to gauge. Adelard might have ded icated his work to Henry merely because he wished to gain the support of the winning faction in the civil war. However, the troubadour Daude de Pradas, in his compendium of falconry, states that he used 'a book of King Henry's' for the passages which come from Adelard's treatise on hawking.[88] Moreover, the *De opere astrolapsus* formed a natural complement, if not a sequel, to Adelard's *Natural Questions*, since the two works are respectively concerned with the higher and the lower worlds, they are both avowedly based on Arabic learning, and they travelled together in one of the two complete manuscripts of the *De opere astrolapsus*.[89] In the course of the *De opere astrolapsus* Adelard refers the Duke to his translations from Arabic of the astronomical tables of al-Khwārizmī and of Euclid's *Elements* for matters not discussed in the *De opere*. Therefore, the dedication of the *De opere astrolapsus* to Henry brings with it the possibility that several works of Adelard were known to Henry. Might Adelard have been involved in Henry's education earlier in his life?

Henry, as we have seen, was in Bristol between 1142 and 1144. Bristol is not far from Bath, but during this period Bath was a royal stronghold, and the bishop (Robert of Lewes) was a staunch supporter of King Stephen. There is, however, another piece of evidence that brings us into Adelard's circle and possibly into that of the young Henry: that is, references to Adelard and a certain 'Alfred', in the glosses of a manuscript written in English

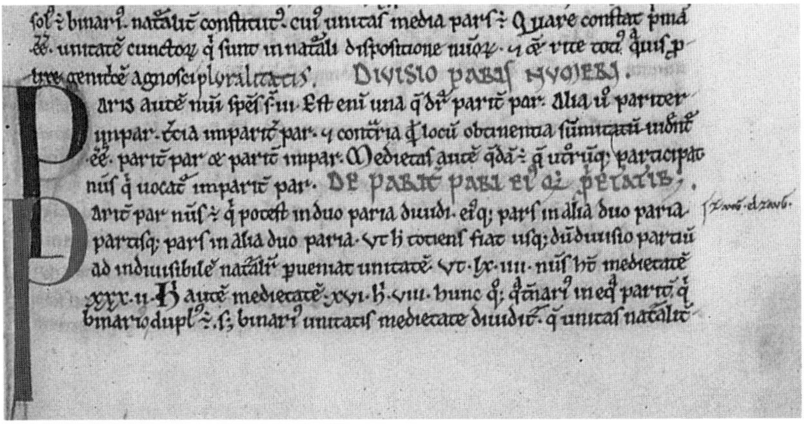

FIG. 16. Oxford, Trinity College, 47, fol. 50r. Arabic glosses to Boethius's *De arithmetica*. The words 'zaug el zaug' are Arabic (*zauj al-zauj*) for 'evenly even' (Latin: 'pariter par'), one of the categories of numbers discussed by Boethius here and by Euclid in *Elements*, VII, def. vi. However, none of the extant Latin translations of the *Elements* retain the Arabic terms here.

and Norman hands in the 1140s.

Christopher Baswell has sketched the character of a 'magister Alvredus' who owned three twelfth-century manuscripts of West Midlands origin, consisting of Virgil's works, the *Panormia* (the well-known legal text of Ivo of Chartres), and Gilbert of Poitiers's commentary on the Pauline Epistles. He proposes that this 'magister Alvredus' is the abbot of the Augustinian house at Haughmond in Shropshire from ca. 1163–70 whom Henry, after he had become king, referred to as having once been his 'nutricius' or 'tutor'.[90] Now, it is tempting to think that this Alfred belonged to a group of West Midlands scholars who were working in Adelard's circle. The hint towards this is provided by MS Oxford, Trinity 47. This manuscript of Adelard's literal translation of Euclid's *Elements* and the *commentum*-version of the *Elements* with references to Adelard's 'intelligence', also includes Boethius's *De musica* with glosses quoting Adelard's opinion.[91]

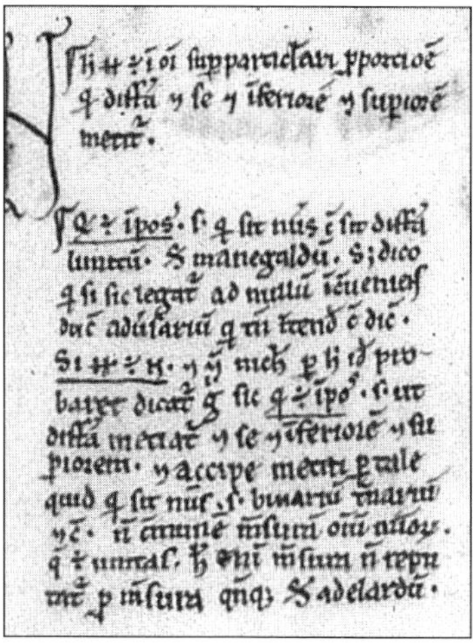

FIG. 17. Oxford, Trinity College, 47, fol. 87v. Glosses mentioning the opinions of Adelard and Alfred.

One of these contrasts the views of Alfred and Adelard (Fig. 17):

> Note that there are two lines of ink according to Alfred, so that there should be between the *meses* a blank space signifying a tone, as there is between other notes, but Adelard rejects this in the previous note.[92]

It is reasonable to think that these glosses are written by students or colleagues of Adelard and Alfred. The experimental and incomplete way in which the *commentum*-version of Euclid's *Elements*, which draws on Adelard's literal translation, has been written in this manuscript, also suggests the works of pupils of the master.[93]

But it must be noted that these new texts and the Arabic glosses have been added to a manuscript of texts on logic, arithmetic and music whose nearest relatives are in Thierry's *Heptateuchon* in Chartres. And the first gloss to Boethius's *De arithmetica* includes mention of the 'formae nativae' which is a distinctive element of the teaching of Bernard of Chartres, William of Conches's teacher.[94]

As in the case of the *Dragmaticon* and the *De opere astrolapsus* so here we have the meeting of influences from Chartres and

England, with the additional factor of a name – Alfred – which is also that of a tutor of Henry. Moreover, MS Trinity 47 seems to represent the beginning of an attempt to put together a codex containing the texts of the seven liberal arts similar in conception to the *Heptateuchon*, and is certainly appropriate for the education of a king.[95]

By the time Adelard dedicated his *De opere astrolapsus* to Henry he was already at the end of his career. Arabic studies had become established in England, and he was one of the people principally responsible for this. Before continuing to investigate Duke Henry's interest in Arabic learning, we ought to go back to the source of Adelard's knowledge of these studies, and see how they developed, especially in the area of Bristol and Bath, further up the Severn Valley, and along the Welsh Marches.

In the first lecture it was shown how certain Arabic doctrines had arrived in England, perhaps already before 1066, via the monastic and cathedral schools of France and Lotharingia. These were instructions concerning the construction and use of the astrolabe, Hindu-Arabic numerals on the abacus counters, and certain astrological doctrines, which accompanied works on arithmetic, rhythmomachy, music, geometry, and the computus. These works continued to be copied in the twelfth century, as we have seen, but were joined by works which came from Arabic Spain (and perhaps Sicily and the Middle East) by more direct roots. The beginning of this new phase is marked by the arrival in England of the Spanish Jew turned Christian, Petrus Alfonsi.[96]

Petrus Alfonsi was educated in an Arabic milieu in Huesca, then part of the Muslim kingdom of Saragossa, and in 1106, ten years after the city's conquest by the Christians, he was baptised. Just as the first involvement of Latin scholars with Arabic science in the late tenth century reflects the renovation of the study of astronomy in Córdoba at the time, so do Petrus's interests reflect the strong interest in mathematics in the court circles of the Saragossan royal family – the Banū Hūd – in the late eleventh century. To this, however, must be added an interest in Arabic texts on natural science and medicine which had not been a feature of the earlier period of transmission in Spain.

Petrus had something to offer to students in the West: lessons in astronomy. This he advertised in his letter to the 'Peripatetics of Francia' in which he decries the low level of astronomical knowledge in Latin Christendom, and emphasises the importance of such knowledge: for medicine, for forecasting the weather, for knowing when eclipses will occur, and other purposes. He promises two things: that he will teach the subject, and that he has books (specifically astronomical tables). The only evidence that anyone took up his offer comes from England. For, in a text on predicting eclipses written before 1120, Walcher, the prior of Great Malvern (whom we have already met as an abacist and a user of the astrolabe), refers to Petrus as 'magister noster'; he describes the whole text as 'the opinion of Petrus the Hebrew, known as "Anphus", about the lunar nodes, which lord Walcher prior of the church of Malvern translated into the Latin tongue'.[97]

It is likely that the prior and the former Jew worked together in England, because Petrus is also described in one manuscript as the doctor of King Henry I.[98] Moreover, the text was copied into a manuscript that was written in Worcester Cathedral Priory, just a few miles from Great Malvern: Oxford, Bodleian, Auct. F.1.9 (the 'Worcester manuscript'). In England too a student skilled in Latin (most likely Walcher himself) helped Petrus to make a Latin version of the astronomical tables of al-Khwārizmī, which Petrus had brought from Spain. In the two manuscripts that survive, chapters have been added to the 'canons' (instructions for use) from a version of the same tables of al-Khwārizmī made by Adelard of Bath. The research of Raymond Mercier suggests that the same Arabic manuscript was used for both versions.[99] Adelard's version immediately follows Walcher's 'translation' of Petrus's opinions on the lunar nodes in the same Worcester manuscript (Plate 3).

The presence of al-Khwārizmī's tables in Worcester was a matter of some pride to the annalist John of Worcester (whose hand is in the Worcester manuscript). He records under the year 1138 that: 'lest the work which is called *Ezich* in the Arabic language, and which a man of the most subtle knowledge, Elkauresmus by name, composed concerning the course of the seven planets and arranged in order, should be consigned to oblivion, I have decided to record when and on what day and on what hour of day the first month of the Arabic year began'.[100]

The most economical explanation for the two Latin versions of the tables is that Petrus had a manuscript of the tables, and taught both Walcher and Adelard in the West Midlands of England. Walcher's terminology is different from Adelard's, and is closer to that of the astrolabe corpus which he knew well, and to the works of Bede; he does away with all Arabic terminology, and the version of the tables on which he is presumed to have collaborated with Petrus converts all the values to the Roman calendar. Adelard, on the other hand, is more ready to accept Arabic terminology and retains the Arabic calendar.

This may be because, unlike Walcher, he has learnt Arabic. For, whereas Walcher does not say what language he translated the opinions of Petrus from (and most likely they were speaking a common vernacular Norman French), Adelard takes full credit both here, and in other works that I shall mention, for translating directly from Arabic. If the Arabic manuscript of al-Khwārizmī's tables was available in the West Midlands for him to translate, then I see no reason why the other Arabic texts Adelard knows were not also there (in fact, one manuscript would have been sufficient).[101] Adelard himself refers on several occasions to his 'Arabic masters',[102] and his own students appear to have been equally conversant with Arabic jargon. What I am suggesting is that Petrus Alfonsi, and perhaps other Arabic-speaking Jews or former Jews collaborated with Adelard and his circle. They may have had a few Arabic manuscripts of their own, but much of the translation was done orally, through the Arabic scholars reading out the texts and translating. In the course of this collaboration not only Arabic technical vocabulary, but also several Arabic phrases and common expressions and jingles were used. The evidence is in the surviving Latin manuscripts, and these are what we shall look at.

First of all, we may note that Adelard retains Arabic phrases in the spells in the book of talismanic magic of Thābit b. Qurra that he translated (*Liber prestigiorum*).[103] For example, Adelard translates Thābit's instructions on how to make a talisman for a wife who wishes to regain the love of her husband, prescribing that an image of a most beautiful woman should be made, and bound to the talisman of the man; rings of Venus and the Sun are to be painted, whilst one says the following prayer:

> O fount of honour, joy and light of the world! Mix together the loves of these two people, o spirits, using your knowledge of mixing, and being helped towards this end by the greatest power and the might of *al-malik al-quddūs wa al-ḥayāh ad-dā'ima* (which Adelard interprets as 'the king, the holy and eternal life'), and by the power of him who moves the heavenly circles, giving to them *nūr wa 'iyān* (i.e., 'light and illumination') over this lower world.[104]

One might say that an unknown, exotic, language was appropriate for spells. But Arabic is also used widely in the copy of Adelard's translation of al-Khwārizmī's tables in the Worcester manuscript. As in the astrolabe texts dicussed in the first lecture, so in these tables Arabic terminology is retained, and highlighted by being written in red ink (Plate 3).

This retention of Arabic terminology could be attributed to an inability to find appropriate Latin terms. But that can hardly be the reason in the case of the additions of whole sentences in Arabic, and, in particular, of Arabic jingles, in the margins of the manuscript. The first occurs on fol. 103v:[105]

kulelach.uueli.
kemithl.elhileli.
fi kemelen.wanuczeni.

A modern Arabic transliteration would look like this: 'kull al-aḥwāli ka-mithl al-hilāli fī kamālin wa-nuqẓāni' ('all the states are like those of the [full] Moon in its fullness and waning'). The second fragment of verse occurs on fol. 127v of the same manuscript:

Cullel.kauuekib.
kumna.fiscerafehu.

ille otarit.[106]
hine.unxi.ademu.

i.e., 'kull al-kawākib qumna fī ashrāfi*hā* illā 'Uṭārid ḥīna unshi'a ādamu' ('all the planets were in their exaltations except Mercury when Adam was born').

Both these verses show some influence of Spanish Arabic (e.g., the *imāla* or tendency towards narrowing the long 'ā' to 'ē'). They have a regular stress pattern which is compatible with the *rajaz* metre,[107] and vowel-rhyme (assonance) at the ends of the phrases.[108] The first verse has, in addition, a strict rhyme of two syllables within the first half of the verse. For Arabic or Latin speakers these verses would serve the purpose of memorable jingles, and hence be parallel to the verses on the astrolabe stars and the names of the abacus counters mentioned in the first lecture.

In the early manuscripts of Adelard's translation of Euclid's *Elements* almost every Latin term is given its Arabic equivalent in the margin. Moreover, there are phrases in the margin, sometimes expressing grammatical points, such as 'al-muḥīṭ, yuḥīṭ, al-mumāss, yamāss', illustrating the difference – for an Arabic speaker? – between 'continens, continet' and 'contingens, continget'; at other times giving common expressions, such as 'awwalan wa-awwalan' 'gradually', and 'fi nafsihimā' 'by themselves'.[109] Similarly, in Adelard's translation of an introduction to astrology by Abū Ma'shar, the Arabic terms are written both in the margin and over the Latin translations (Fig. 18).

FIG.18. Sloane MS 2030, 84v. The Arabic terms for the '16 states of the planets' in Adelard's translation of Abū Ma'shar's *Abbreviation of the Introduction to Astrology*, eds C. Burnett, K. Yamamoto and M. Yano, Leiden, 1994, p.110.

The use of Arabic was continued by Adelard's pupils. A certain 'Joannes Ocreatus' is credited in British Library, Royal MS 15.A.XXVII, with writing a version of Euclid's *Elements*, which is, in fact, very similar to that of the *commentum*-version in MS Trinity 47, and includes notes on Arabic words (Fig. 19). Another 'Ocreatus' (possibly 'H. Ocreatus') writes about the new Saracen way of doing arithmetic.[110] The essence of it is that numerals have place value: 2 in the units position is 2, but in the tens position is 20, in the hundreds position is 200 etc., just as the abacus counters derive their values from their places. For this way of doing arithmetic al-Khwārizmī had used Hindu-Arabic numerals which already had place value. This form of calculation

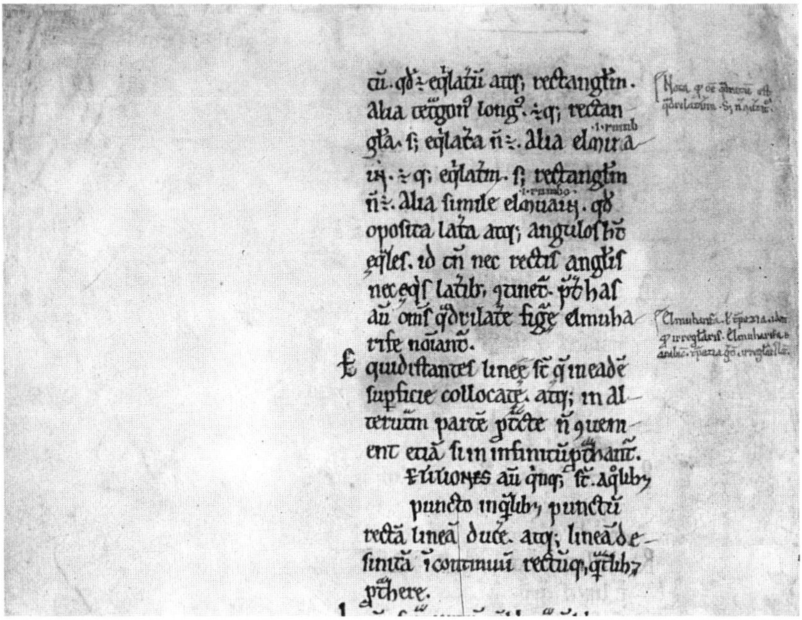

FIG. 19. Royal MS 15.A.XXVII, fol. 1v. The version of Euclid's *Elements* attributed to 'Joannes Ocreatus'. Note the gloss giving Arabic, Greek and Latin equivalents for the trapezoid: 'Elmunharifa arabice, trapezium grece, irregularis latine'.

became so much identified with al-Khwārizmī that it acquired his name, and was called the algorism. But it was not necessary to use Hindu-Arabic numerals for calculation with place-value. Ocreatus used the nine Roman digits. Thus he does not mention al-Khwārizmī, but refers to his work 'Helcep Sarracenicum', i.e., 'Saracen calculation' (*helcep* being a transliteration of the most common Arabic word for 'calculation': *al-ḥisāb*). But in this text, which is not a translation, certain Arabic phrases have crept in: e.g., we find the sentence 'cum vellem ducere finaph<s>ihi'[111] = 'when I would like to multiply (the number) *fī nafsihi*' which happens to be the Arabic for 'by itself', and, indeed, the procedure described is that of finding the square (Fig. 20). All this suggests an oral milieu of teaching, with a considerable amount of familiarity with the Arabic language.

So this is the situation when Adelard dedicated his *De opere astrolapsus* to Henry Plantagenet. If we trust the words of Adelard's preface, we must believe that Duke Henry already had a desire to 'understand the opinions of the Arabs'. His eagerness may have been stimulated by the references to *studia Arabum* in Adelard's *Natural Questions*. Adelard bids the young duke to be bold enough to wish to understand not only the things that Latin writings contain, but also the opinions of the Arabs concerning the sphere and the course and movements of the planets. The text is full of references to his Arabic masters. He names his authority for the astrolabe: Maslama al-Majrīṭī. Naturally, he does not expect the duke to understand Arabic, and when he quotes Arabic terms, he gives Latin interpretations, which are often lacking in the more technical works that we have just mentioned.[112] Most striking is the fact that he translates into Latin the jingle from the Worcester manuscript about all the planets being in their exaltations except Mercury when Adam was born, and sets it in a larger context, which is worth quoting, because it includes a remarkable plea for religious tolerance:

> Hence it comes about that in the first clime (i.e., near the Equator), they say, the home of philosophers (*domus philosophica*) has its natural position. For there all seeds spring up spontaneously and the inhabitants always do the right thing and

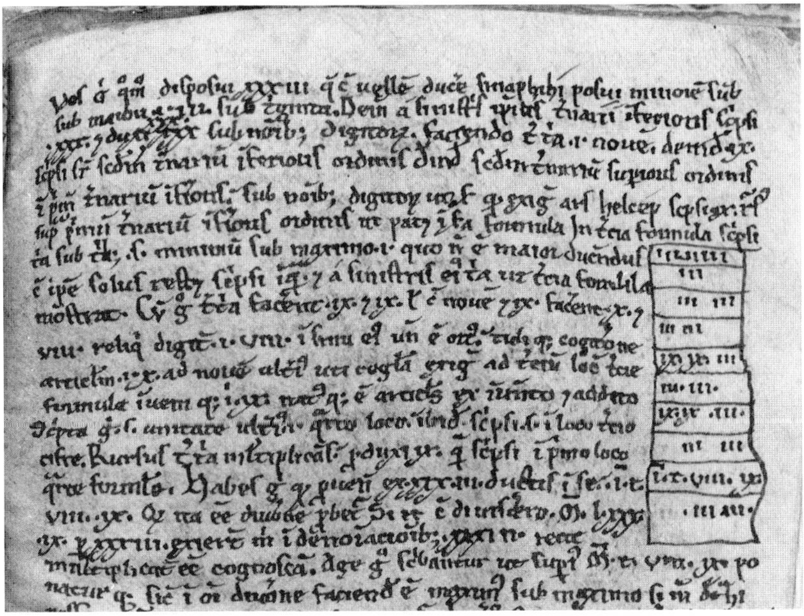

FIG.20. Cashel, GPA Bolton Library, Medieval MS 1, p.115. A page from the *Helcep Sarracenicum* of Ocreatus. Note the Arabic phrase 'finaph<s>ihi' i.e., *fī nafsihi*, in the first line and the use of Roman numerals as digits with place value in the calculation of 33 × 33.

> speak the truth. Obeying only God first, and the spirits of the planets second, and sharing everything in common, they live happily. Following the way of nature and reason only, when they meet anyone of any religion (*lex*) in their everyday life they greet him with this motto: 'iyyāka <wa> dābba', which means 'beware of the Beast'. According to the Arabs, this is the fatherland that the philosophers were granted. It is here that, when all the planets except Mercury were in their exaltations, when the Creator willed and the condition of the heavens was encouraging generation, the first man was born.[113]

'Iyyāka <wa> dābba' ('aiekadeb') is indeed an Arabic phrase meaning 'beware of the Beast'. The Dābba is mentioned in the

Koran (xxvii, 82) and is the archetypal Beast, equivalent to the Thērion of the Apocalypse of St John.[114] After the day of Judgement it will rise from out of the earth and set upon the foreheads of people the signs 'believer' or 'ungodly'. Presumably this greeting is an injunction to make sure you are marked out as a believer. When combined with the statement in Adelard's dedication that philosophers should be kings or kings philosophers, this certainly provides an agenda for kingship: Henry should be a philosopher, philosophers act rightly and speak the truth; they follow natural justice and reason, and are tolerant of people of any religion. Moreover, the avowed authority for this agenda is not the classical *auctores* (even though *we* can recognize Plato here[115]), nor the Church Fathers, but the Arabs.

★ ★ ★ ★

The young Henry did not have a monopoly on Arabic learning. A partisan of King Stephen, who had learnt how to draw up horoscopes, and knew the introduction to astrology by al-Qabīṣī which had been translated by John of Seville, was responsible for drawing up the horoscopes for the King's party in the years around 1151 (Fig. 21);[116] for they include a prediction that the army of Normandy will not come (23 August 1151), and that the king is obliging his barons to pay homage to his son (16 September 1151), and they mention that the duke of Normandy has died (i.e., the death of Geoffrey Plantagenet on 7 September 1151; the horoscope was cast 8 days later). One horoscope adds that the king can do nothing without his astrologer, another refers to a contract ('consortium') made between a lord and his disciple 'dei servus', which, if it is not simply a reference to his piety, looks very much like the Arabic name 'Abdallah (= 'servant of God').

However, 1150, the date of the dedication of the *De opere astrolapsus*, is significant because it marks the arrival of another stage of Arabic astronomical influence in England, and one perhaps not unconnected with Henry Plantagenet. For '1149 completed years' is the phrase used to describe the starting point of two sets of Latin instructions for the use of tables originally

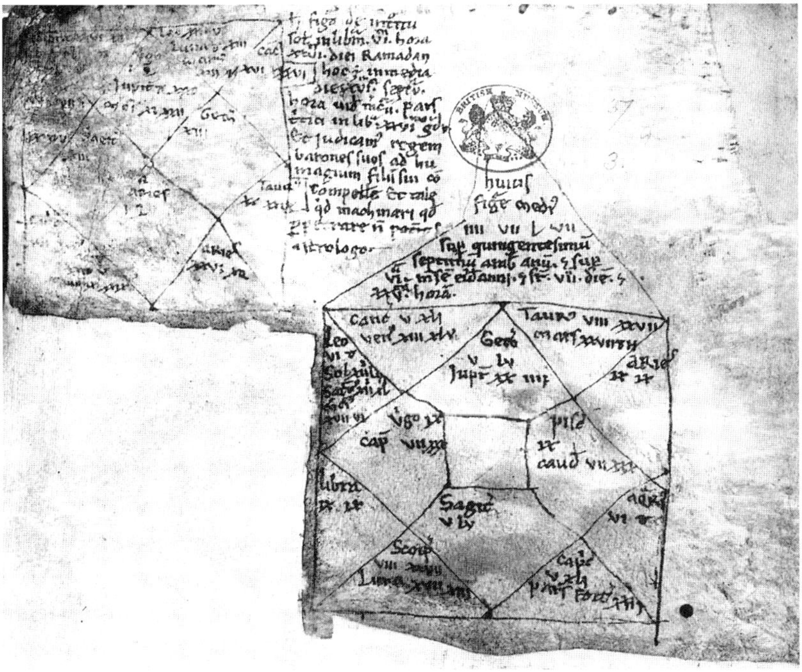

FIG.21. Royal MS App. 85, fol.1v. Two horoscopes cast for a sympathiser of King Stephen. The first reads: 'Hec figura de introitu Solis in Libram .vi.^{ta} hora .xxvi.^{ti} diei Ramadan, hoc est in media die .xvi.^{ma} Septembri, hora videlicet Mercurii, pars tritici in Libra .xxvi.^{to} gradu. Et iudicamus regem barones suos ad humagium filii sui [com]compellere, et tale quid machinari quod perpetrare non poterit sine astrologo.'

drawn up by the learned Jew Abraham ibn Ezra for the meridian of Pisa in 1143; this implies that the instructions were made in 1150.[117] Among Jewish scholars Abraham ibn Ezra is known as a poet, scientist, Biblical exegete and a sage.[118] From his own Hebrew writings and the testimonies of other Jewish scholars, we know that he was born in Tudela on the banks of the river Ebro between 1089 and 1092, and spent the first part of his life mainly in his native land, with occasional visits to North Africa. But in 1140 he left his home and travelled extensively, visiting Jewish communities throughout Europe. For a while he was in Tuscany; he was in Pisa and Lucca in the mid 1140s. He is then known to have been in Béziers and the neighbouring Narbonne,[119] and at the end of the decade he visits several places in Northern France, including Rouen, the capital of Normandy, and Dreux in the Royal Demesne and only 20 miles from Chartres. It is in France in the late 1140s that he wrote a series of astrological books in Hebrew.[120] In 1158 he spent several months in London.[121]

To these facts from Hebrew sources can be added the Latin testimony of one of the sets of instructions for the use of the Pisan tables written in the year 1150: those in Arundel MS 377. For they are headed: 'Tractatus magistri Habrahe de tabulis planetarum' ('Treatise of master Abraham concerning the tables of the planets'), and at the end of the preface is written: 'these tables were composed according to the longitude of Pisa, which is 33 degrees from the West. But the longitude of Angers is about 24 degrees from the West, and the same is true for Winchester' (Fig. 22). Angers was, of course, Geoffrey of Anjou's capital, and Winchester had powerful symbolic importance to English rulers, and thus the references to these two cities in this order nicely trace the itinerary of Duke Henry from the court of his father to his triumphal entry into England in 1154.[122] Moreover, the Arundel manuscript contains, precisely, copies of William of Conches's *Dragmaticon* and Adelard's *De opere astrolapsus*, the two works composed for Duke Henry. The same work of Adelard's is accompanied by the other set of instructions for Ibn Ezra's Pisan tables in MS Cambridge, Fitzwilliam Museum, McClean 165, to which we shall return. Abraham ibn Ezra's involvement in the Arundel and Fitzwilliam manuscripts is indicated by another factor: namely, the presence of 'figure indice' ('Indian numerals') in the manuscripts.

What we call 'Arabic numerals' do not correspond to the kind of numerals that the Arabs adapted from the Indians. The latter became established in Baghdad and the Eastern part of the Islamic world from the eleventh century onwards, and are now

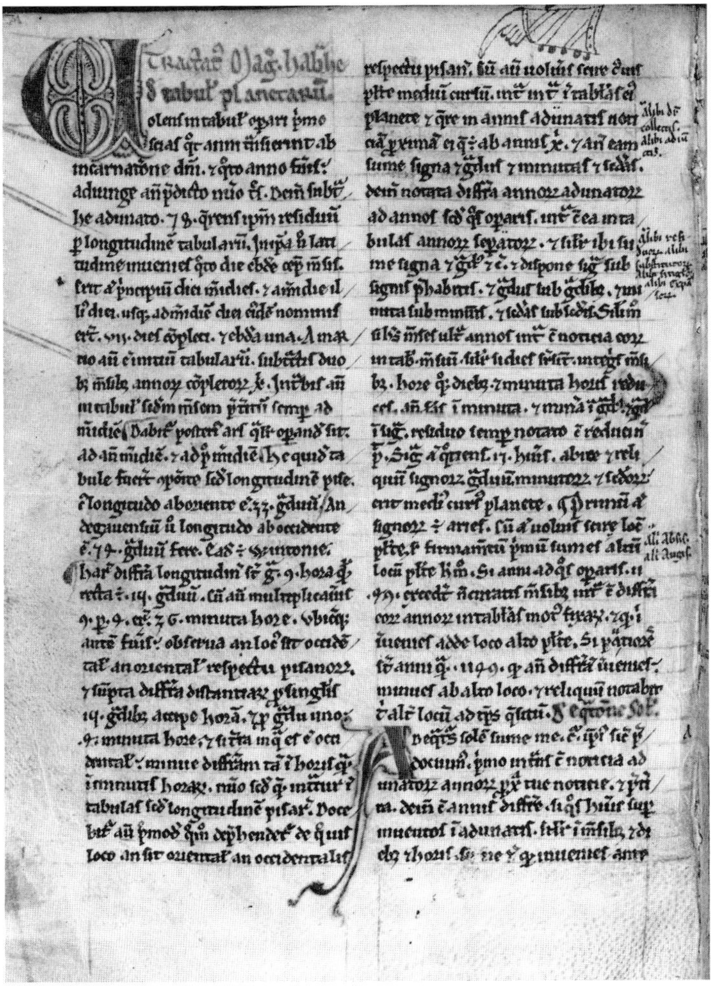

FIG. 22. Arundel MS 377, fol. 56v. The beginning of the 'Tractatus magistri Habrahe de tabulis planetarum' with the mention of Pisa, Angers and Winchester.

the conventional form used in Arabic script. Our Arabic numerals derive from a peculiar variant of this form, that developed in al-Andalus and became common (to the extent that Hindu-Arabic numerals became common) in the Maghreb (i.e., al-Andalus and North Africa west of Egypt). The Arabs called this Western form 'al-ḥurūf al-ghubārīya' ('the dust characters') in distinction from 'al-ḥurūf al-hindīya' ('the Indian characters'). In Latin texts the latter term was retained: 'figure indice', but the 'dust characters' were called the 'figure toletane', i.e., they were particularly associated with Toledo and the translations made there.[123] Now, only in a few manuscripts of the twelfth and early thirteenth centuries are the 'figure indice' retained. The majority of these are manuscripts of the Latin works of Abraham ibn Ezra. One of these manuscripts is Cotton MS Vespasian A. II.

Cotton MS Vespasian A. II is a composite manuscript of miscellaneous material. The relevant codex within this manuscript (fols 27–40) consists of works by Rudolph of Bruges and Abraham ibn Ezra, and nothing else;[124] both these scholars were in Béziers in the 1140s. The works of Abraham are his *Book of the Foundations of the Astronomical Tables*,[125] the most complete of the introductions to the Pisan tables, written before 1154,[126] and his work on the astrolabe, which is also found in the Arundel manuscript. That of Rudolph is a text on the astrolabe, in the tradition of 'Ptolemy and his follower Maslama'.[127] The numerals in the two works of Abraham are written entirely with 'figure indice' (Fig. 24).

The 'figure indice' did not catch on, and soon became unintelligible. In some of the manuscripts in which they are used we find a key to their significance and/or the 'figure toletane' written above them.[128] In the Arundel manuscript the 'figure toletane' are not used in Abraham's text, but the key survives (Fig. 23), on the page before the beginning of Abraham's work, which strongly suggests that the Arundel text is a copy of a manuscript in which Abraham's text was written with 'figure indice' with a key at its end, such as Bodleian, Digby 40.

The second manuscript containing both instructions for the use of the Pisan tables and Adelard's *De opere astrolapsus* –

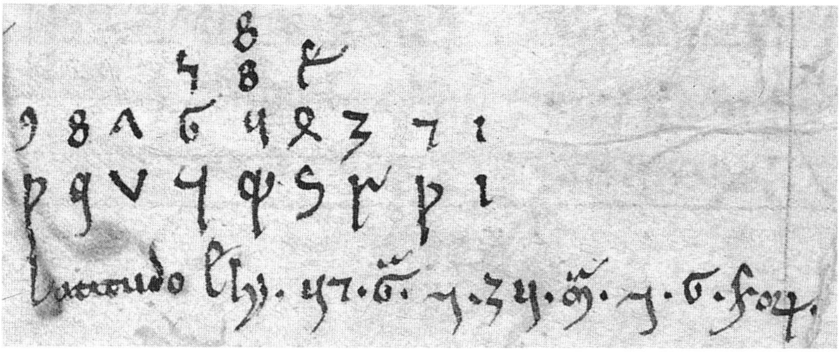

FIG.23. Arundel MS 377, 56r. The 'figure indice' (lower set) and 'figure toletane' (upper set), with alternate forms for '4', '5' and '6'. Under this is the description of the latitude of Ely, using the *figure toletane*. 'latitudo Ely. 52 gr(aduum), et 35 m(inutiorum) et 6 secundorum'.

Cambridge, Fitzwilliam Museum, McClean 165 – retains the 'figure indice', and includes a second feature which indicates a Continental origin: namely, texts associated with Raymond of Marseilles. The first of these is the *Liber cursuum planetarum VII*, which is the rather literary introduction to astronomy and instructions for the use of tables for Marseilles, written in 1140, the second, the book of astrological judgements (*De iudiciis*) ascribed to Ptolemy which Raymond used as a basis for his own *Book of Judgements*; the Fitzwilliam manuscript includes a commentary on the same Pseudo-Ptolemaic work. Now, the Pseudo-Ptolemaic judgements may have come to the realms of King Henry by the same route as the Pisan tables and their instructions. For, the earliest manuscript of this text – Harley MS 5402 of the twelfth century – also includes some instructions in a mixture of Italian and Latin, which seem to be an adaptation of the Pisan tables for the meridian of Lucca in 1160,[129] and the 'figure indice' typical of the Latin works of Abraham ibn Ezra (Fig. 25). The next earliest manuscript of the *Iudicia* is Paris, Bibliothèque nationale, lat. 16208, which also includes Raymond of Marseilles's works and a fragment of the Tables of Pisa, and has on its front fly-leaf a horoscope cast by 'Abraham iudeus' for a boy born in 1136 at Béziers. If this is not Abraham bar Ḥiyya,

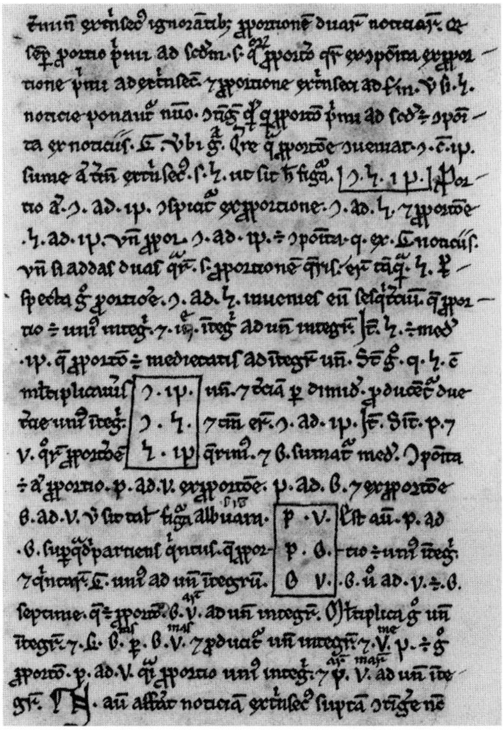

FIG.24. Cotton MS Vespasian A.II, fol.29rb. 'Figure indice' in a manuscript of Abraham ibn Ezra's *Book of the Foundations of the Astronomical Tables*.

the Jewish scholar from Barcelona,[130] it could hardly be anyone other than Abraham ibn Ezra.[131]

Of the Arundel and Fitzwilliam manuscripts of the *De opere astrolapsus* the Fitzwilliam alone includes Adelard's dedication to Henry and the 'figure indice' in Ibn Ezra's text. The instructions for the use of the Pisan tables, drawn up in 1150, are the latest work in the manuscript.[132] This manuscript could very well, then, represent the astronomical material in the court of the Plantagenets.

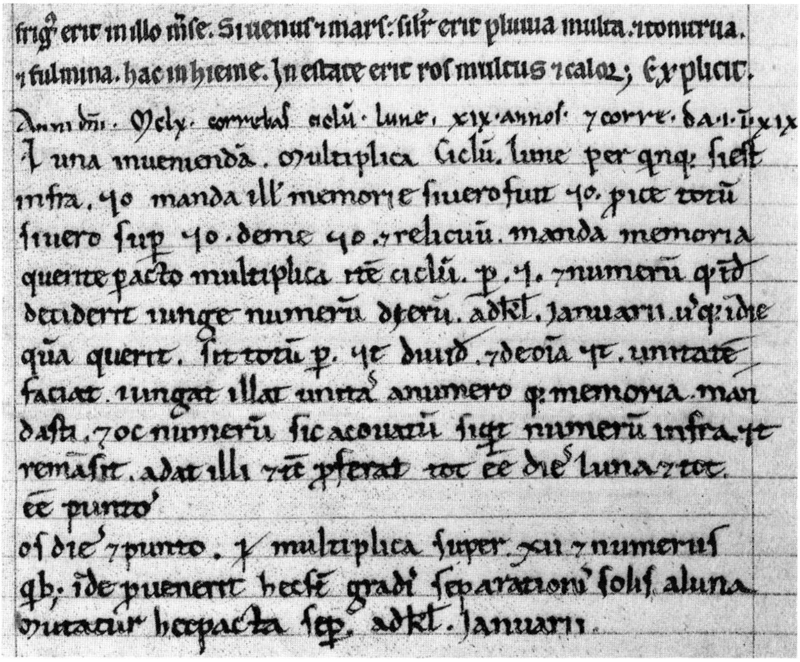

FIG.25. Harley MS 5402, fols. 69r. Instructions for finding the position of the Moon. Note the year 1160 in Roman numerals in the third line, and the use of the 'figure indice' for writing '60' in the sixth and seventh lines.

The Arundel manuscript, on the other hand, shows a later stage in the copying of this same material. It omits the dedication to Henry and the cosmological part of Adelard's *De opere astrolapsus*.[133] Variants for the astronomical *termini technici* have been copied by the scribe in the margins of Abraham's text: these

FIG.26. (Following pages) Arundel MS 377, fols 86v–87r. Roger of Hereford's adaptation of the tables of Raymond of Marseilles for the meridian of Hereford. Note the confusion still caused by the '0': in the second sequence of 28-year intervals in the first column it has been left out in the date 12<0>4.

Alt' Toleti. xl. g'd.
Alt' Sol ap Heford
i tpre hiemali. xiiij.
g'd. i Sign. xxxviij. g'.
Solsticiali. lxij. Lati
tudo. lij. g'd. Dies
max'. xvi. hor' et
bisse. Longit'. xxiiij.
g'd. Salt' sol' i me
dio signor.
Capricorni. xiiij. g'.
Aquari'. xx. g'd.
Pisces. xxx. g'd.
Aries. xlij. g'd.
Taur'. lij.
Gemini. lx.
Cancer. lxij. g'd.
Leo. lvij. g'.
Virgo. xlvij.
Lib'. xxxiiij.
Scorpi'. xxiiij.
Sagitt'. xvij.
H sed m'dic
Heford et Astla
bin dicta s't.

MAnni collecti omniu' planetar' compositi
magistro Rogero s'c' annos d'ni ad medi
noctem Herfordie. anno ab i'carnatione
d'ni. m. c. lxx. viij. p' eclipsi q' magist'
Heford eod' anno. I futuro m'iecto un' f
tagit eclipsis sol' et lune. ap' Aren.
.xij. dies Sept'. et .xv. horas. et .qr.
Ap' Massilia' p' .xij. dies. Sept'. et .xij. h
tas. et .qr. m. Ap' Toleti p' .xij. dies
et .xi. horas. et .l. m. Ap' Heford p'.
dies Sept'. et .xi. horas. et .xxx. m. Vn
Aren et Massilia. s't. xlv. g'd. s. tres
s't Massilia' et Toleti. xvi. g'd. s. ho
et q'ntadecima uni' hore. I't Massil
et Heford. xxi. g'd. s. hora et due q'nte.
Toleti et Heford. v. g'd. s. xx. m. hore
q' s't p'stcia uni' hore. Vn cu' sit lo
gitudo Aren. xx. g'duu'. et Toleti lo
gitudo. xxix. g'duu'. Massilie. xlv. h
ford. xxxiiij. g'duu'. e' g' remotio Hefo
ab Arin. lxvi. g'duu'. s. iiij. horaru'
et tcia et q'ntedecime uni' hore. E't lo
gitudo uniu'cuiusq' civitatis s'tce ap' oc
d'ntem ab Arin remoto ipsi ab occident
ipi' Arin. id est ab extremitate orientis e'
occidente. Vn tardi' f' p'dicta opra s't
dia nox ap' Heford. q' ap' alias p'nomi
tas civitates. Vn adduxu' etiam ad me
u' motu' ei' f' p'dicta opra. q'd et facti
i p'senti tabula s'c' mo' Massilie. tu' p
a'nos d'ni. et bissextos. tu' pp' m'ses ro
manos. Malui'm eni' h' q' a'nos ara
et eor' m'ses pp' difficultate' eor'. eo q'd
i'usitata sint ap' n'rates.

Solis Anni	S	G	M	Sa
Radix	9	9	13	54
1320	9	9	2	6
1348	9	8	51	18
1376	9	8	40	30
1404	9	8	29	42
1432	9	8	18	54
1460	9	8	8	6
1488	9	7	57	17
1516	9	7	46	28
1544	9	7	35	41
1572	9	7	24	53
1600	9	7	14	5

Lune Anni	S	G	M	Sa
Radix	9	16	19	14
1320	1	10	54	34
1348	5	5	29	54
1376	9	0	5	13
1404	0	24	40	33
1432	4	19	15	53
1460	8	13	51	13
1488	0	8	26	33
1516	4	3	1	53
1544	7	27	37	13
1572	11	22	12	33
1600	3	16	48	53

here lune Anni	S	G	M	Sa
Radix	7	5	21	57
1320	9	0	56	44
1348	10	26	31	31
1376	0	22	6	19
1404	2	17	41	6
1432	4	13	15	53
1460	6	8	50	40
1488	8	4	25	28
1516	10	0	0	15
1544	11	25	35	2
1572	1	20	9	49
1600	3	15	44	36

Saturni Anni	S	G	M	Sa
Radix	3	14	57	24
1320	2	27	6	55
1348	2	9	16	28
1376	1	23	25	59
144	1	3	35	31
1432	0	15	45	3
1460	11	27	54	35
1488	11	10	4	7
1516	10	22	13	39
1544	10	4	23	11
1572	9	16	32	43
1600	8	28	42	15

Jovis Anni	S	G	M	Sa
Radix	6	29	53	1
1320	11	9	38	13
1348	3	19	24	25
1376	7	29	10	38
1404	0	8	56	50
1432	4	18	43	1
1460	8	28	29	14
1488	1	8	15	27
1516	5	18	1	39
1544	9	27	47	51
1572	2	7	34	3
1600	6	17	20	15

Martis Anni	S	G	M	Sa
Radix	8	21	21	50
1320	7	10	43	10
1348	6	0	4	30
1376	4	17	25	50
1404	3	8	47	10
1432	1	28	8	30
1460	0	17	29	50
1488	11	6	51	10
1516	9	26	12	30
1544	8	15	34	51
1572	7	4	54	10
1600	5	24	15	39

here veneris Anni	S	G	M	Sa
Radix	4	28	15	43
1390	11	3	27	57
1348	5	8	39	11
1376	11	13	51	26
1404	5	19	4	40
1432	11	24	16	54
1460	5	29	29	8
1488	0	4	41	22
1516	6	9	53	36
1544	0	15	5	50
1572	6	20	18	4
1600	0	25	30	18

here mercurii Anni	S	G	M	Sa
Radix	1	14	50	35
1320	4	17	5	8
1348	7	19	19	41
1376	10	21	34	15
1404	1	23	48	48
1432	4	26	3	22
1460	7	28	17	55
1488	11	0	32	28
1516	2	2	46	2
1544	5	5	1	35
1572	8	7	15	9
1600	11	9	29	42

Capitis Draconis Anni	S	G	M	Sa
Radix	11	10	34	45
1320	5	12	32	57
1348	11	13	31	6
1376	5	20	29	20
1404	11	18	24	32
1432	5	20	25	43
1460	11	22	23	55
1488	5	24	23	6
1516	0	26	20	18
1544	6	28	18	29
1572	0	0	16	41
1600	5	2	14	53

often correspond to Robert of Chester's adaptation of Adelard of Bath's translation of the tables of al-Khwārizmī.[134] Now, Robert was also responsible for drawing up the Pisan tables for London, either in 1150 or in 1170; he revised Adelard of Bath's translation of the tables of al-Khwārizmī, and perhaps was one of the pupils of Adelard who produced the *commentum*-version of Euclid's *Elements* in manuscript Trinity 47.[135] The Arundel manuscript also includes an English adaptation of Raymond of Marseilles's *Liber cursuum*: namely, Roger of Hereford's adaptation of the tables for the meridian of Hereford, made in 1178 (Fig. 26). The only other later addition to the Arundel manuscript is Daniel of Morley's *Philosophia* which will be discussed in greater detail in the third lecture. Suffice to say here that it presupposes a close knowledge of William of Conches's *Philosophia*[136] and Adelard of Bath's works, especially *De opere astrolapsus*, and it was dedicated to one of Henry II's closest associates ('familiares'), John of Oxford, bishop of Norwich.

Daniel takes his account of planetary movement and his diagrams from Adelard's *De opere astrolapsus* (Plate 4). But the remaining Ptolemaic astronomy in his *Philosophia* is from al-Farghānī's *Rudiments of Astronomy*, which had been translated by John of Seville in Limia in Northern Portugal in 1135. A copy of al-Farghānī's work can be found in the Arundel manuscript, immediately preceding Ibn Ezra's explanation of the Pisan tables. On the other hand Daniel takes his astrology from Adelard's translation of Abū Ma'shar's *Abbreviation of the Introduction*, with some additions from the Arabic astrologer's *Great Introduction* translated by Hermann of Carinthia, the teacher of Rudolph of Bruges.[137]

The role of Abraham ibn Ezra, therefore, may have been very significant. Before 1140 he was in Tudela, on the river Ebro; a year later Peter the Venerable found Hermann of Carinthia and Robert of Ketton 'on the banks of the Ebro'.[138] They had probably known Ibn Ezra. That he moved from North Spain to Pisa in the early 1140s is also not insignificant. Pisa at that time was not only a flourishing commercial centre with quarters in cities throughout the Mediterrenean, but (as is becoming increasingly clear) a centre of translation activity, from Arabic as well as from

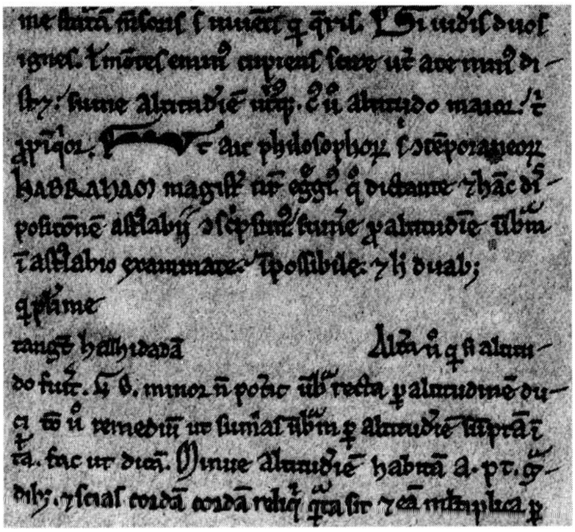

FIG.27. Cotton MS Vespasian A II, fol.40v. The mention of Abraham, the Latin writer's master.

Greek.[139] Ibn Ezra would have been in Pisa at the same time as Burgundio of Pisa, the doyen of the translators of Greek theological, philosophical and medical texts into Latin, who will be mentioned again in the next lecture. But it is also quite likely that he was aware of the Arabic-Latin translations and original works of Stephen of Pisa, who made his translation of the *Kitāb Kāmil aṣ-ṣinā'a aṭ-ṭibbīya*, 'Alī ibn al-'Abbās al-Majūsī's medical compendium, in Antioch. Stephen also used the 'figure indice', and it is possible that they were introduced into the West *via* Pisa.

Then Abraham was in Béziers and the neighbouring Narbonne. In 1143 Hermann of Carinthia was also in Béziers,[140] and Hermann's only known pupil, Rudolph of Bruges, in his book on the astrolabe, uses, as his only example, an observation made in Béziers on 24 April 1144.[141] It cannot be fortuitous that Rudolph's work is flanked by two works of Ibn Ezra in Cotton MS Vespasian A.II. By 1148 Ibn Ezra is in the realms of Geoffrey of Anjou; the mention of Angers in instructions to his astronomical tables in 1150 is surely significant.[142] But the mention of Winchester points towards another country – England, where, after Henry's accession to the throne, Ibn Ezra's presence is also attested. It is unlikely that he was solely responsible for the Latin texts that he wrote in these places. Like Petrus Alfonsi, he probably collaborated with a Latin-writing colleague. In fact, this is indicated at the end of the astrolabe text which occurs in the Arundel and Cotton Vespasian manuscripts (Fig. 27):

> as says Abraham, outstanding among the philosophers of his time, and our master, on whose dictation we wrote this account of the astrolabe.[143]

Who this Latin writer is, is not stated. If Robert of Chester is the same as Robert of Ketton, as has usually been assumed,[144] then his candidature is attractive. For, the reviser of the Pisan tables for the meridian of London would be the same as the scholar whom Ibn Ezra may have got to know many years earlier in the valley of the Ebro. But arguments could be made for another scholar or other scholars participating in this collaboration.[145]

The common factors in the earlier texts copied into Arundel MS 377 – William of Conches's *Dragmaticon*, Adelard of Bath's *De opere astrolapsus*, and Ibn Ezra's instructions for the use of the Pisan tables – are that they are all either addressed to members of the Count of Anjou's family, or mention Angers as the place for which the text is relevant, and they were all written between 1144 and 1150. Thus, it does not seem too far-fetched to refer to these works as texts related to the education of Henry II.

After Henry acceded to the kingdom in 1154, 'philosophers' continued to be attached to Henry's court.[146] For, the two authors whose works have been added to the earlier texts in Arundel MS 377 – Roger of Hereford and Daniel of Morley – were both justices of king Henry.[147] Moreover, from 1154 to 1167 the king's justiciar (i.e., the head of the *Curia regis* and chief judge)[148] was Robert, earl of Leicester, who received the dedication of an adaptation of Raymond of Marseilles's *Liber iudiciorum*, which picks out the astrological judgements especially relevant to medicine.[149] To Robert was also dedicated the *Speculum fidei* of Robert of Cricklade, prior of St Frideswides in

Oxford from before 1141 until after 1171. This includes quotations from Hermann of Carinthia's translation of Abū Ma'shar's *Great Introduction to Astrology*. Robert of Cricklade also dedicated a work to Henry himself – a précis of Pliny's *Natural History* – and makes a point in his preface which is similar to Adelard's in the *De opere astrolapsus*, that it is inappropriate for the king to be ignorant of the different parts of the world of which he rules a large portion.[150] Charles Haskins suggested that Robert of Cricklade could be the 'Roboratus' to whom Henricus Aristippus, working in Palermo, addressed his translation of Plato's *Phaedo*.[151]

Thus we have quite a close-knit set of interconnections, centred on the Court of the King (*Curia regis*) and, within it, especially on the Exchequer, of which Robert, earl of Leicester, was the president. It might not be coincidental then, that the Arundel manuscript we have been discussing, which gathers together the texts associated with the King, comes from the Cathedral priory of Ely, where Richard FitzNigel, Treasurer of the Exchequer from 1158 to 1195, and author of the *Dialogus* on the Exchequer, had been brought up, and where he returned as archdeacon in 1160. His father and predecessor as Treasurer, Nigel, was bishop of Ely until his death in 1169, and his successor was another relative, William of Ely.

Another point to be borne in mind is that the Jewish element in intellectual life in Henry II's England continued to be important. The majority of the indigenous Jews in England were Ashkenazi – i.e., Northern European. Among these was Benedict the 'punctuator' in Oxford, who translated Adelard of Bath's *Natural Questions* into Hebrew.[152] Some Jews or converts from Judaism, however – especially the visitors – were Sephardi (from Spain), and would have used Arabic as their first spoken language, and written it in Hebrew characters (i.e., Judaeo-Arabic): e.g., Petrus Alfonsi and Abraham ibn Ezra. Ibn Ezra's prime reason for coming to England would have been to visit the Jewish communities there, and he dedicated a work (*Yesod Moreh*) to one of them, Joseph ben Jacob, in London. Another Sephardi in England was Solomon ben Isaac, the owner of a seal whose inscription is translated by Joseph Jacobs as 'Solomon ben

Isaac who has donned the turban. May Allah guard him'.[153] Yet another was mentioned in a previous Panizzi lecture by Malachi Beit-Arié, who drew attention to a document in which 'a Jewish creditor living in England recorded payments made to him at the end of the twelfth century by various Englishmen, including three bishops, in areas extending from Bath to Norwich and from Exeter to Winchester'. The owner wrote his records 'in Arabic . . . in Hebrew characters in a cursive Spanish Andalusian type of script'.[154] Members of the Jewish community had frequent contacts with the royal court, through their position as financiers.

Henry II, then, was in constant contact with scholars who had been in Arabic-speaking regions and who had various degrees of competence in speaking, writing or reading the Arabic language. He would have been aware of the reputation Muslim scholars had in the sciences. Adelard of Bath had acknowledged Arabs as his masters.[155] Robert of Ketton quotes Hermann of Carinthia as claiming that al-Kindī is the most reliable authority in astrology.[156] John of Salisbury credits the Muslims as the only people to understand geometry, which they pursue for the sake of astronomy.[157] In 1168 Henry's party threatened that Henry would follow the religion of Nūr ad-Dīn, the sultan of Aleppo, and become a Muslim, if the Pope did not depose Thomas Becket as archbishop of Canterbury. Perhaps this threat could have been taken more seriously at the time than modern scholars are inclined to believe.[158] For, if we follow Adelard's words, Henry had been imbued in philosophy and curious about the *studia Arabum* from his very infancy.

The Beginnings of Oxford University

IN THE LAST lecture I showed how the *studia Arabum* were pursued especially by royal tutors and servants of Henry II, and referred briefly to two justices of the king, Roger of Hereford and Daniel of Morley. In this lecture I would like to start with a closer investigation of the only known work of the latter scholar. Daniel of Morley dedicated his *Philosophia* to John of Oxford, bishop of Norwich from 1175 to 1200 (the dedication probably falls early in this period, as we shall see). Daniel writes:

> When, some time ago, I went away to study, I stopped a while in Paris. There I saw asses rather than men occupying the Chairs and pretending to be very important. They had desks in front of them heaving under the weight of two or three immovable tomes, painting Roman Law in golden letters. With leaden styluses in their hands they inserted asterisks and obeluses here and there with a grave and reverent air. But because they did not know anything, they were no better than marble statues: by their silence alone they wished to seem wise, and as soon as they tried to say anything, I found them completely unable to express a word. When I discovered things were like this, I did not want to get infected by a similar petrification, and I was seriously worried that the liberal arts, which illuminate the Bible, were being skipped over, or read only in exam cribs. But when I heard that

the doctrine of the Arabs, which is devoted almost entirely to the quadrivium, was all the fashion in Toledo in those days, I hurried there as quickly as I could, so that I could hear the wisest philosophers of the world. . . Eventually my friends begged me to come back from Spain; so, on their invitation, I arrived in England, bringing a precious multitude of books with me.

How disappointed I was when I was told that even here the liberal arts were mute and Aristotle and Plato were forgotten in favour of Smith *versus* Jones.[159] But then I heard that such studies were flourishing in Northampton, and, not wanting to be the only Greek among Romans, I set out for that town. But I was on my way there when I met my lord and spiritual father, John, bishop of Norwich, who showed me great honour and respect (in keeping with his character) and was pleased that I had come.

As happens when friends meet after a long absence, I was repeatedly questioned by my lord the bishop about the wonderful things in Toledo and the teaching there. His last question, about the the movements of the celestial bodies, lead the talk round to astrology. He mentioned, for instance, that some things on this earth seem to be subservient to their superiors, as if under a bond of fealty. Because the shortness of time did not allow me to answer these questions sufficiently, I decided to present the following treatise for his scrutiny. Its first book is about the lower part of the universe, its second about the higher. I beg the reader earnestly, that, just because everything is set out in black and white, he should not despise the simple and clear opinions of the Arabs, but should note that Latin philosophers make heavy weather of these subjects quite unnecessarily, and, through their ignorance, have put forward figments of their imagination veiled in obscure language, so that their unsteady floundering in this subject might be covered by a blanket of unintelligibility.[160]

Two things must be noted here: first, that Daniel claims to be bringing a large number of books from Toledo to England; secondly, that he stopped *en route* for Northampton. He never says he reached Northampton. Whichever way he was going – he may, for example, have been following one of the routes of the English pilgrims from Santiago de Compostella, disembarking at

Bristol or Southampton – it was likely that he passed through Oxford, which, as Richard Southern points out, was 'a centre of communications in the Midlands' and 'one of the main crossings of the Thames'.[161] This hypothesis is supported by two facts: first, Daniel's bishop, John, was himself a native of Oxford and we know that he was in the city at least twice in the period of his bishopric.[162] But secondly, and more importantly, the new books that Daniel brings with him (if we may judge from the sources of his *Philosophia*) are found precisely in Oxford very soon after his return to England. It is not my intention to discuss again here the shadowy beginnings of Oxford as an institution of learning – suffice to say that the earliest testimonies are in the last decade of the twelth century – nor to give a roster of the 'magistri' that are attested as having taught there.[163] Rather, I wish to look at the texts and the manuscripts that were known in Oxford at the time that it starts to take shape as a university – an aspect which has been less explored.

What were the books that Daniel of Morley brought with him from Toledo? The only way to answer this question is to look at the sources of his own *Philosophia*. First, it is modelled very closely (and consciously) on Adelard of Bath's *Natural Questions* and *De opere astrolapsus*. Thus both the first book (on the lower world) and the second book (on the higher world) begin with Daniel's claim that he is giving the 'doctrina Arabum' ('teachings of the Arabs') or the 'rationes Arabum' ('the logical arguments of the Arabs'), echoing Adelard's claim that the *Natural Questions* give the result of his investigation of the *studia Arabum*, whose hall-mark is reason. When Daniel starts to discuss the 'constitution of the world', he recalls the opening of Adelard's *De opere astrolapsus*:

> Because a wise resident should not be ignorant of the composition of his own house, concerning this spatious house which is the home of everything, I shall write in Latin what I learnt in the Toledan language from Ghalib the Mozarab.[164]

Adelard had used the same metaphor of the house, and, similarly, had written 'I shall write in Latin what I have learnt in

Arabic'.[165] When one adds the fact that Daniel copies whole passages from Adelard's *De opere astrolapsus* and his translation of Abū Ma'shar's *Abbreviation of the introduction to astrology*, one finds that Daniel had a knowledge of Adelard's works which went far beyond that of any other scholar. He uses Adelard as his starting point – literally, for his very journey to Toledo is in imitation of Adelard's 'seven-year' wanderings in pursuit of the *studia Arabum*. But he adds new sources to those known to his predecessor. Two of these are texts on the science of the stars, which were not translated in Toledo and could have already arrived in England by other routes (e.g., with Robert of Ketton or Abraham Ibn Ezra):

1) Al-Farghānī's *Rudiments of Astronomy*, translated by John of Seville and Limia, in Limia in Portugal on 11 March, 1135, which, as we have seen, was already in Arundel 377, with Adelard's *De opere astrolapsus* and Abraham ibn Ezra's works.
2) Hermann of Carinthia's translation of Abū Ma'shar's *Great Introduction to Astrology*, translated in 1140, which was already known to Robert of Cricklade, prior of St. Frideswide's Augustinian Abbey in Oxford until after 1171.

But another two were translations from Arabic of works concerning Aristotle's natural science. The first is the 'book on describing the reason why the sciences came into being' (referred to conventionally as *De ortu scientiarum*), the second is 'the book of the heavens and the world' (*Liber celi et mundi*).

The *De ortu scientiarum* is clearly a translation from Arabic, but the Arabic original has not been found. In Latin manuscripts it is either unattributed or attributed to Avicenna (once) or Alfarabi (once). Daniel makes Aristotle the author. *De ortu scientiarum* gives a rational reason for the coming-into-being of each of the sciences, from mathematics, through physics, to the divine science or metaphysics. For example, under the heading 'about getting to know the reason according to which natural science came into being' the anonymous author writes:

> I say that since substance sometimes reddens, sometimes pales, sometimes lasts for a longer, sometimes for a shorter period of time, sometimes increases in size, sometimes decreases, sometimes comes into being and sometimes passes away, sometimes is sick, and sometimes is well, there had to be a science which showed all of this, i.e., through which we might arrive at knowing how such changes take place, and what their causes and occasions are, and how we might remove those causes that are harmful and encourage those that are beneficial, and this was the science of natures. . . . When we enquire into its roots, we will find four elements, fire, air, water and earth, which are the mass of substance contained under the circle of the Moon, and from whose qualities – heat, cold, moisture and dryness – arise the accidents in substance and acting-upon and suffering. From these four roots, together with the four mathematical sciences already described, there came into being the science of what falls under the circle of the Moon.[166]

The short treatise ends by giving arguments for the immutability of the heavens, from which it is deduced that they are made of a fifth 'matter', other than fire, air, water and earth. The whole treatise is a blueprint for the Arabic Aristotelian division which arose out of the teaching in Alexandria in late antiquity, though the author does not mention by name Aristotle or any of his works (or those of anybody else). It also must be mentioned that the treatise is both totally Islamic, especially in its description of God,[167] and also provides a physical justification for astrology and natural magic. Thus we find, immediately after the account of the origin of natural science, just quoted, the following subdivisions of the science:

> The parts of this science, according to the words of the first wise men, are eight: astrological judgements, medicine, natural necromancy, talismans, agriculture, navigation, alchemy (which is the science of turning things from one species into another) and perspective.[168]

Daniel quotes most of the last section of the *De ortu scientiarum* for his proofs that there are five 'natures' and that the heavens are unchangeable. Moreover, the purpose of his *Philosophia*, as hinted at already in the preface, is to give the Arabs' justification of astrology. Daniel cautiously disowns these opinions,[169] as Adelard too had done,[170] but is eager to quote from new astrological works and to join the debate about astrology's validity. Moreover, he reproduces the same eight divisions of natural science that are found in the *De ortu scientiarum*,[171] but this time makes them divisions of astrology, and replaces 'imagines', the word used for talismans in the *De ortu*, with 'prestigia', the word used by Adelard in his translation of Thābit ibn Qurra's treatise on magical talismans.

The second text is even more important for Daniel. For, almost a third of his *Philosophia* consists of quotations from the *Liber celi et mundi*.[172] This work, again, has not been identified in an Arabic manuscript, but it is possible that it is the same as the 'sixteen questions on Aristotle's *De caelo*' which, according to the tenth-century Arabic bibliographer, Ibn an-Nadım, were written by Ḥunain b. Isḥāq.[173] Ḥunain was the leading figure in the enterprise by which Greek philosophical and medical texts were turned into Arabic in ninth-century Baghdad. The *Liber celi et mundi* follows the arguments of Aristotle's *De caelo* closely, and refers to several other texts by Aristotle. However, the author departs from Aristotle in one significant respect. Whereas Aristotle had argued for the eternity of the world – a position incompatible with both Islam and Christianity – our author states that the world had a beginning and will end.[174]

Daniel refers to the *Liber celi et mundi* by name twice, without giving an author. But on several occasions he uses the work without acknowledgement: e.g., to supplement the arguments in the *De ortu scientiarum* for the immutability of the heavens.[175] Moreover, he does not hesitate to refer to the books of Aristotle which are quoted in the *Liber celi et mundi*, as if he had consulted them directly: 'Aristotiles in libro de auditu naturali' (i.e., the *Physics*) and 'Aristotiles in libro de sensu et sensato' (i.e., on *Sense and Sensation*).

Daniel is the first scholar outside Toledo to use the *De ortu scientiarum* and the *Liber celi et mundi*. Given their prominence in his *Philosophia*, it is, too, very likely that these are two of the books which he boasted that he had brought back from Toledo. In one manuscript of the *Liber celi et mundi*, the translators are named as 'Gundisalvo et Johanne', and preliminary investigation of the style and terminology suggests that Gundissalinus and John of Spain are meant.[176] The translator of the *De ortu scientiarum* is not named in the manuscripts, but the text was known to Gundissalinus, who quotes from it the same eight divisions of 'natural science' as does Daniel,[177] and the *De ortu scientiarum* accompanies Gundissalinus's works in the manuscripts.[178]

Gundissalinus was an archdeacon of Segovia cathedral who was resident in Toledo, and, in collaboration with a Jewish scholar called 'Avendauth', and with perhaps an Arabic speaking Christian (i.e., 'Mozarab') called 'John of Spain' produced translations of several parts of the *Shifā'* of Avicenna, Algazel's *Maqāṣid al-falāsifa* (Algazel's summary of Avicenna's Aristotelian philosophy), and the 'fount of life' of Avicebron.[179] Gundissalinus's choice of texts was perhaps influenced by Avendauth, for this must be Abraham ibn Dāūd, the Jewish philosopher who fled from Córdoba as a result of the persecution of the Jews by the Almohads,[180] the religiously-inspired Berber movement based in Marrakesh, who had overrun al-Andalus in 1147. Ibn Dāūd had settled in Toledo by 1160, and here he wrote works on the reconciliation of philosophy and Judaism, the history of the Jews in Spain, and astronomy. There is extant a letter by Avendauth, in poor Latin, addressed to some important person (perhaps the archbishop of Toledo himself) advertising the fact that he intends to translate the *Shifā'*, and accompanying a specimen of this translation, preceded by versions of an Arabic biography of Avicenna, and Avicenna's own preface to the work.[181] It is important to note that Avicenna did not write commentaries on Aristotle's texts, but wrote his own philosophy in the Aristotelian tradition. This line was continued by Gundissalinus, who, again, wrote no commentaries, but original works closely based on the translations he and his team had made.

In his *Philosophia*, Daniel does not refer to Gundissalinus, but only to Gerard of Cremona (1114–87), the most prolific translator working in Toledo, whose interests, and whose approach to his sources, were very different from those of Gundissalinus, as we shall see. However, the only text in which Gerard was involved, mentioned by Daniel, is Ptolemy's *Almagest*, which, according to Daniel, Ghālib ('Galippus') the Mozarab interpreted for Gerard, and Gerard 'latinized'.[182] Now, we are told by his students that it was specifically to look for the *Almagest* that Gerard came to Toledo.[183] Thus, Daniel probably encountered Gerard early in his translating career, and this would suggest, too, that the *Philosophia* must be dated closer to the beginning of John of Oxford's bishopric (1175) than to its end (1200). At any rate, Daniel talks of Gerard in terms of someone who is still alive; thus writing before 1187, the date of Gerard's death. There is no doubt that Daniel was in Toledo, probably in the 1160s, and that the *De ortu scientiarum* and the *Liber celi et mundi* originated from Toledo.

What is new about these texts, from the point of view of Latin readers, is that (aside from the question of the eternity of the world), they are thoroughly Aristotelian. For the first time in this story of the transmission of Arabic learning that is the subject of these lectures we have texts conveying Aristotelian natural science. Daniel was aware of this, too. For he takes every opportunity to drop the name of 'Aristotle' even in the case of dubious attributions. But the question remains as to whether he brought these books to Oxford.

That Daniel met his patron, John of Oxford, *in* Oxford is only a likely hypothesis. But that hypothesis is strengthened by the fact that the principal text that Daniel advertises – the *Liber celi et mundi* – was known to Alexander Nequam who was teaching in Oxford by 1190, and until about 1197, when he became an Augustinian canon at Cirencester. He had a particular interest in natural science, and an enthusiasm for the new works of Aristotle, and on medicine. The new texts of Aristotle that he knows (the *Metaphysics* and *Ethica vetus*) were translated from Greek into Latin by James of Venice and Burgundio of Pisa, and are also extant in the manuscripts copied at, or brought to, Mont St-Michel, the Benedictine Abbey in Normandy – these manuscripts containing our earliest surviving copies of these texts.[184] Nequam might have got to know them in Paris, where he records meeting Urso of Calabria, the Salernitan master who promoted medical texts translated in Italy both from Greek and from Arabic into Latin.[185] The one text that is *not* found in the Mont St-Michel manuscripts, or anywhere else on the continent until after Nequam's time, is the *Liber celi et mundi*. However, it is precisely this text which appears, in the company of the other Aristotelian texts that Nequam knows, in a codex of booklets bound together in ca. 1200 at the Abbey of St Albans, where Nequam had been brought up and with which he continued to have close ties in his later life. This manuscript is now Bodleian Library, Selden supra 24.

Aside from the *Liber celi et mundi*, Nequam knew two further texts translated from Arabic. The first is the *De plantis*, the work on botany attributed to Aristotle, translated by Alfred of Shareshill who dedicated a work to Nequam (we shall come back to this). The second is the *De causis* – a translation of an Arabic text on metaphysics based on Proclus's *Elements of Theology*. This is also in the St Albans manuscript where, significantly, it is called 'the *Metaphysics* of Avendauth'. No other manuscript gives it this title, which closely associates the text with Gundissalinus's circle.[186]

A more thoroughgoing use of texts from Gundissalinus's circle can be seen in another Oxford man who dedicated a work to Nequam. This is John Blund, who, between 1200 and 1204, wrote a work *On the soul*, which appears to reflect a lecture course based on questions. Blund was teaching in the Faculty of Arts at Oxford from ca. 1200 to 1209, when the university was closed because of riots. He was described by Henry of Avranches in 1232 as

> the first man to investigate deeply the books of Aristotle, when the Arabs had recently handed them over to the Latins, and the man who had lectured on Aristotle first and with the most renown in both Oxford and Paris.[187]

This is not strictly accurate. Like Nequam he uses the Greek-Latin translations of Aristotle made by Burgundio of Pisa and James of Venice – adding that of the *De anima*, also by James[188]

– and medical texts of Salernitan origin. But his use of Arabic sources is nevertheless extensive, and it is confined almost entirely to two texts translated by Gundissalinus and his team: sections of Avicenna's *Shifā'* and Algazel's summary of Avicenna's philosophy, the *Maqāṣid al-falāsifa*. Whether these translations of Gundissalinus and his colleagues were also in the 'multitude of books' brought by Daniel from Toledo remains to be proven.

The second scholar whose work Nequam knew is Alfred of Shareshill, or 'Alvredus Anglicus', who dedicated to Nequam an original text *On the movement of the heart*. The main purpose of this text was to justify the Aristotelian position of making the heart the primary seat of the soul, rather than the brain, which was the Galenic position held by doctors (*medici*). Alfred provides another link between the university teachers and the 'royal servants' discussed in the second lecture. For he dedicated another text – the *De plantis* – to Roger of Hereford, the royal justice who had revised the astronomical tables of Marseilles for the meridian of Hereford. But, whereas Daniel of Morley and John Blund can be seen to belong to the philosophical tradition of Avicenna and Gundissalinus, Alfred represents a different tradition. That is, the tradition of translating authoritative works for a teaching curriculum, and providing commentaries for them.

This tradition can be traced in an almost unbroken line stemming from the schools of Alexandria in late Antiquity, and dividing into two branches, one continuing in Greek in Constantinople and Magna Graecia, the other, in Syriac and Arabic dress, passing through Baghdad into al-Andalus. To this tradition belong James of Venice and Burgundio of Pisa who prepared literal translations of Aristotle's texts, and, in several cases, either translated the Greek glosses already accompanying the texts, or provided their own explanatory glosses.[189] This approach was presumably encouraged in the French schools, and especially in Paris, where glossing or commenting upon authoritative texts had become the main vehicle of instruction in the Faculty of Arts. This approach was certainly that taken by Gerard of Cremona, who may well have been inspired by the example of James and Burgundio in his native land, before moving to Toledo in the mid-twelfth century to commence a translating programme of clear purpose – with rigorous consistency.

Gerard would have found this programme set out in precise detail, in a work of the philosopher known among the Arabs as 'the second philosopher' (i.e., the second Aristotle): Abū Naṣr al-Fārābī. Alfarabi wrote a book called *On the classification of the sciences* which describes, in order, the sciences of language, mathematics, natural science and theology or metaphysics. Both Gerard and Gundissalinus made Latin versions of this book. It is much more comprehensive than the *De ortu scientiarum* known to Daniel of Morley. In particular, it prescribes the textbooks appropriate for each of the divisions of science. If one looks at the translations of Gerard of Cremona it seems that he was methodically working his way through Alfarabi's list of titles, to make sure that the Latins would have a complete set of authoritative texts for philosophy.

For, in natural science, Gerard translated the first three titles on Alfarabi's list – Aristotle's *Physics*, *De generatione et corruptione*, and *De caelo*. He then embarked on the fourth title, the *Meteora*, but completed only the first three books. Here he stopped. Whether he knew that Henricus Aristippus had already translated the fourth and last book of the *Meteora* from Greek, in Sicily, is not clear.[190] In any case, he was probably prevented by his death in 1187 from completing the programme.

It is exactly at this point that Alfred of Shareshill takes over. He adds Aristippus's translation of the fourth book of the *Meteora* to Gerard's translation of the first three, and, reading that 'the book of minerals' is the next on Alfarabi's list, but finding no work on the topic by Aristotle himself, he takes the chapters on minerals in the *Shifā'* of Avicenna, and puts them at the end of the *Meteora*. This composite *Meteora* is first found in the same St Albans manuscript which is closely associated with Nequam, where we read in the colophon of the work:

> The book of *Meteora* of Aristotle of which the supreme philosopher Gerard of Lombardy translated three books from Arabic into Latin, but Henricus Aristippus translated the fourth

from Greek into Latin. The last three chapters were translated by Alfred the Englishman of Shareshill from Arabic into Latin.[191]

The proof that Alfred had Alfarabi's list in mind is in his first gloss to the *Meteora* which reads:

> The title of the book is etc. . . . It must be noted that Alfarabius in his book On the sciences, in the chapter on the natural sciences, says: 'The fourth enquiry is concerning the principles of actions and passions and those things which are only elements, without considering what is composed from the elements, and it is in the first three books of the book *Meteora*.'[192]

The next title on Alfarabi's list is 'the book on plants'. Again, no such work is known to have survived on this topic, written by Aristotle himself. But from an early period Nicholas of Damascus's work on the same subject, in that it included much of Aristotle's lost work on plants, was incorporated into the Aristotelian canon, and it is this work that Alfred translated from Arabic.

The fact that Alfred continued Gerard's programme of translation strongly suggests that Alfred himself spent some time in Toledo, probably towards the end of Gerard's life, or just after his death. This hypothesis is strengthened by the presence of several words from a Spanish vernacular in his translations. It is probably here that he studied with a certain Master Salomon Avenraza, 'the most famous Jew and leader of modern philosophers',[193] who has not been identified, but who would have played a similar role for Alfred to that of Abraham ibn Dāūd for Gundissalinus, and, before that, Petrus Alfonsi and Abraham ibn Ezra for the translators in the first half of the century.

To the translations that Alfred made, he wrote commentaries. Given the distribution of his dedications, the likelihood is that he was teaching these texts in Oxford, and it is noteworthy that the only manuscript to preserve his glosses on the *Book of Minerals*, is, once again, the St Albans manuscript.

Both aspects of Alfred's work – the production of translations and commentaries – were continued by a Britisher, the colourful and enigmatic Michael Scot.[194] Scot's origins are obscure. At one stage in his life he was invited to become archbishop of Cashel in Ireland, but refused on the grounds that he did not know the local language; he could as easily have come from Scotland as from Ireland. He first appears as a canon in the cathedral of Toledo in 1215, and it is here, in the years before 1220, that he completed the translation of the last remaining untranslated text in Alfarabi's list of works on natural science: the book on animals (i.e., the Arabic combination of three books on zoology by Aristotle). After 1220 Michael left Toledo for Italy, and eventually served the emperor Frederick II Hohenstaufen in Palermo, where he translated, or superintended the translation of, several large commentaries on Aristotle's natural science and metaphysics composed by Averroes. Averroes had died in Cordoba as recently as 1198; the large commentaries were his last works, and it is significant of the degree of communication between scholars separated by political and religious boundaries, that Michael Scot was already translating these works in the early thirteenth century. What is curious is that it is precisely those works in the corpus of natural science that have commentaries by Alfred – the *Meteora* and the *De plantis* – that do not receive a Latin translation of a commentary by Averroes. Either Alfred's commentaries on these works were used because no commentary by Averroes was available, or Alfred's commentaries were regarded as being sufficiently full and literal for there not to be a need to translate anything by Averroes.[195] It is also significant that the first use of the commentaries of Averroes translated by Michael Scot was made by an English scholar: Robert Grosseteste.[196]

Grosseteste bridges the gap between the intellectual activity in the West Midlands (discussed in the second lecture) and Oxford University.[197] He is first attested as part of Bishop William de Vere's household in Hereford between 1186 and 1198. From 1225, and possibly already before that,[198] Grosseteste was teaching in Oxford. Between 1228 and 1232 he wrote a commentary on the eight books of Aristotle's *Physics*, and added (to all appearances as if he had acquired the book only when he had almost finished his commentary) two sentences from Averroes's

Large commentary on the Physics, whose author he refers to as 'Averroys, commentator Philosophi videlicet Aristotelis'.[199] Around the same time it is evident that he gets to know the commentaries on *De caelo*, *De anima* and the *Metaphysics*, the last of which he virtually summarises in his own works on *Potency and Act* and *On the movement of the celestial bodies*. After he became bishop of Lincoln in 1235 he concentrated on Greek and on moral philosophy, but his activity even in this is not isolated from the Arabo-Latin current of the Toledan translators. For, the last of the Toledan translators, Hermann the German, knew Grosseteste's version of Aristotle's *Ethics* when he came to translate the Arabic commentaries on the *Rhetoric*.[200]

In the early thirteenth century a curriculum of natural science became established. It consisted of Aristotle's *Physics*, *De caelo*, *De generatione et corruptione*, the *Meteora*, *De anima*, and the so-called *Parva naturalia*, and was completed by works not by Aristotle: Qusṭā ibn Lūqā's *On the difference between the spirit and the soul*, Nicholas of Damascus's *De plantis*, and the *De causis*. The two works which are additional to the titles mentioned by Alfarabi are Qusṭā ibn Lūqā's *On the difference*, which was already in one of the Mont St-Michel manuscripts, and travelled from an early date with medical texts from Salerno;[201] and the *De causis*, whose use by Nequam we have already noted.

To this corpus of natural science Aristotle's *Metaphysics* was often added. This collection of texts is conventionally called the 'corpus vetustius' ('the older corpus [of natural science]') to distinguish it from a 'corpus recentius' ('the younger corpus') of basically the same texts but with the Arabic-Latin translations replaced by translations made directly from Greek where possible. The main elements of this corpus were already in the minds of the translators, especially Gerard of Cremona, Alfred of Shareshill and Michael Scot, as we have seen. It did not include the *De animalibus* ('On animals'), either because of the length of the work, or because the translation was made too late. For the completed corpus may have existed already in Paris in 1215 where the reading of (or lecturing on) Aristotle's works 'on natural philosophy and metaphysics' in the arts faculty was banned. But many of the earliest manuscripts of the *corpus vetustius* are

English, and it is in Oxford in the late 1230s and the 1240s that the first full commentary based on teaching courses was compiled: that of Adam of Buckfield.[202]

Adam of Buckfield commented on virtually all the books of the *Corpus vetustius*. For the *Meteora* and *De plantis* he used Alfred of Shareshill's commentary as his starting point; for the other works of Aristotle he used Averroes. Buckfield's commentaries exist both as continuous texts (with Aristotle's text appearing as *lemmata*) and as marginal commentary. Sometimes excerpts from his commentaries are added to another marginal commentary which we may call 'the Oxford gloss',[203] of which there are some examples in the British Library.

The reason for calling a series of glosses which occur in English manuscripts of the second half of the thirteenth century 'the Oxford gloss' is that, in one of these manuscripts – Royal MS 12.G. II – the following note has been inserted after the official mark of ownership:

> quem librum scripsit Henricus de Renham et audivit in scolis Oxonie et emendavit et glosavit audiendo
>
> 'Henry of Renham wrote this book and attended lectures on it in the schools of Oxford, and emended it and glossed it in the course of the lectures'.

The manuscript belonged to the Cathedral Priory of Rochester. Since the volume was brought to Rochester in the time of a Prior John (possibly John of Renham, prior 1262–83; 'Rainham' is a village just outside Rochester), the course was heard at Oxford in the last decades of the thirteenth century. In a comment Henry of Renham has inserted on the first folio the coherence of the course is indicated.[204]

The earliest manuscript to contain a complete copy of the *Corpus vetustius* with the 'Oxford gloss' and some commentaries of Adam of Buckfield is Vatican Urb. lat., 206, written by English hands before 1253. But there are a few more manuscripts in the British Library of the *corpus vetustius* with the Oxford gloss, which cannot be precisely dated.[205] They vary in the

FIG.28. Royal MS 12.G.V, fol.4r. The beginning of Aristotle's *Physics*. Aristotle is shown teaching a group of students. One has his book in front of him, and is perhaps 'emending it and glossing it', as Henry of Renham had done.

amount of annotations they include, and in the degree of care with which they have been prepared.

As in Adam of Buckfield's commentaries, so here, we find that the 'Commentator' – i.e., Averroes – is the principal (if not only) authority cited for most of the genuine Aristotelian texts (Fig. 29). But for the *Meteora* and *De plantis*, Alfred is the principal or sole authority. Averroes is most frequently cited simply as the 'Commentator'; but this term is occasionally used for Alfred too,[206] who sometimes becomes an Arab himself in the manuscripts: for his name is confused with that of Alkindi.[207] In the case of Qusṭā ibn Lūqā's *On the difference between the body and the soul*, no commentary by either Averroes or Alfred appears to have been known to the Oxford masters (Fig. 30). The Oxford gloss, however, contrasts Aristotle and the philosophers with the

FIG.29. Harley MS 3487, fol.4r. The beginning of Aristotle's *Physics*. Note '9^{or}' = 'commentator' (i.e., Averroes) at the beginning of the first marginal note; on this manuscript see M. Camille, 'Illustrations in Harley MS 3487 and the Perception of Aristotle's *Libri naturales* in Thirteenth Century England', in *England in the Thirteenth Century: Proceedings of the First Harlaxton Symposium on English Medieval Studies*, ed. M. W. Ormrod, Woodbridge, 1986, pp.31–44.

'medici' (whose doctrines are given in *On the difference*) and refers to 'Alfred of Shareshill in *On the movement of the heart*' (Fig. 31).

It is against this background of a fixed curriculum in natural science and metaphysics, consisting of texts and commentaries translated from Greek and Latin, that one must consider the eccentric views of Roger Bacon. Roger Bacon had lectured on the *libri naturales* of Aristotle in Paris at exactly the same time as Adam of Buckfield was lecturing in Oxford, but it was his 'private research' after 1247 – whether in Paris or Oxford is unclear – which led to his most characteristic views.[208] He had a knowledge of Arabic texts unparalleled by anyone outside Spain itself.

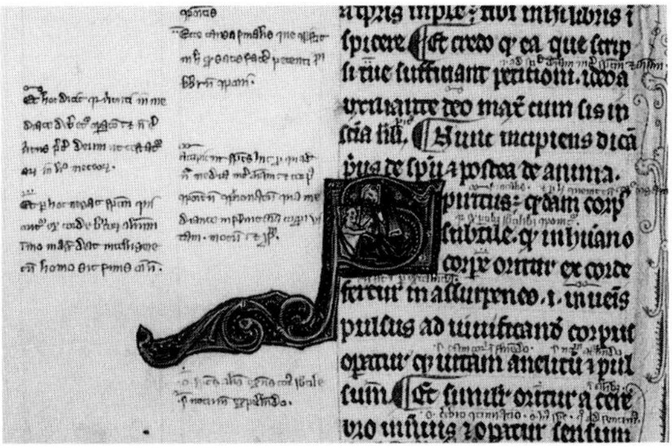

FIG.30. Harley MS 3487, fol.202v. From Qusṭā ibn Lūqā's *On the difference between the spirit and the soul.* A doctor feeling the pulse of a sick man.

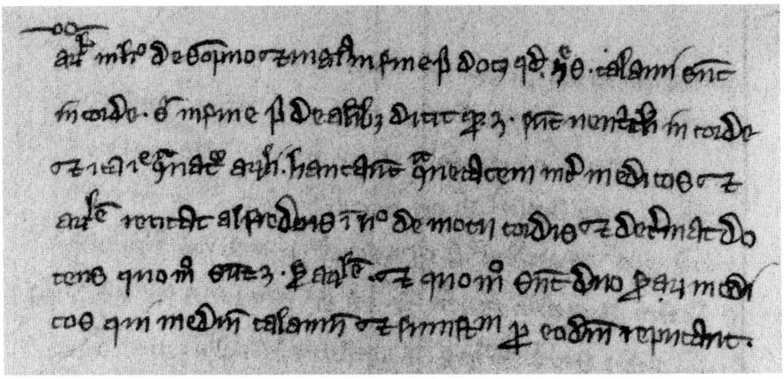

FIG.31. Harley MS 3487, fol.202v. A marginal comment in Qusṭā ibn Lūqā's work points out the difference between Aristotle and the author of *On the difference*, who represents the medical tradition; the comment includes a reference to Alfred of Shareshill's *De motu cordis*: 'Ar(istotiles) in Libro de sompno et vigilia in fine primi docet quod tres calami sunt in corde, sed in fine primi De animalibus dicit quod tres sunt ventriculi in corde et ita ille contrariatur Aristotili. Hanc autem contrarietatem inter medicos et Aristotilem recitat Alfredus in Libro de motu cordis.'

For example, he knew Avendauth's translation of the introduction to the *Shifā'* of Avicenna, which survives in only two manuscripts, and the preface to Algazel's *Maqāṣid al-falāsifa*, in which Algazel explains that he is setting forth a résumé of the opinions of the philosophers only to refute them, which is found in only one manuscript.[209]

Bacon's private studies resulted in his plans to reform the whole curriculum of the Schools and to replace it with a *scriptum principale* of his own that would present the whole of learning (*integritas sapientiae*). He described this new plan in three propaganda documents that he addressed to his friend, Pope Clement IV, in 1267: the *Opus maius*, the *Opus minus* (being a summary of, and introduction to, the whole work), and the *Opus tertium*, being a kind of appendix to the whole. He sent all three texts to the pope, with an accompanying letter.

One of the main things he advocates for the new curriculum is the study of languages: Hebrew and Greek for theology, Arabic and Greek for philosophy. He does this because he finds completely unsatisfactory the translations of Gerard of Cremona, Alfred of Shareshill, Michael Scot and Hermann the German (to whom he adds, on one occasion, the Greek-Latin translator largely responsible for turning the *Corpus vetustius* into a 'corpus recentius', William of Moerbeke).[210] He criticises them all for knowing neither the subject-matter nor the two languages involved – not even Latin. He quotes from his own conversation with Hermann the German, who admitted not knowing logic – which would seem to be necessary for understanding the works of rhetoric and poetics that he was translating – and who said that he had had help from Muslims (*Saraceni*) in Spain.[211] Only Boethius and Grosseteste receive some qualified praise, the first for knowing the languages, the second for knowing the subject-matter.[212] The only remedy was to learn the original languages.

Bacon's advocacy for learning Arabic was taken up by Ramón Llull, the indefatigable campaigner for the conversion of the Muslims. He successfully argued for the implementation of language-learning in the universites at the Council of Vienne in 1312, where, for the first time officially, the Church ordained that lectureships in Arabic, Hebrew, Greek and 'Chaldee' (i.e.,

Aramaic) should be established in each of the universities of Paris, Oxford, Salamanca and Bologna, and at the papal curia. Although this ruling was frequently appealed to by supporters of language learning in the following centuries, it was only sporadically put into practice, and where that happened, only Greek and Hebrew were taught. Neither Bacon nor the Council of Vienne had any perceptible effect on studies of the Arabic language. The Arabic texts continued to be read in Latin translation, being subject to more and more detailed commentary and discussion, but without there being a perceived need to go back to any Arabic originals. With rare exceptions in the intervening period, it was only in the late fifteenth century, and in Italy, with personalities such as Girolamo Ramusio and Leo Africanus, that scholars started to handle Arabic texts directly again.

Epilogue

So we come to the end of the story of the introduction of Arabic learning into England. I hope I have demonstrated how pervasive the presence of Arabic learning was in medieval England. However, I cannot claim to be the first to have revealed these facts. For someone else has been over the same ground before. This is Gerard Langbaine, who was born in 1609 and was successively bateller, taberdar, fellow and provost of Queen's College, Oxford.[213] He was the Keeper of the Archives of the University, and during the Commonwealth he tried hard to uphold the rights of the University and of the episcopacy, against strong opposition from the government. He was one of the few royalists who kept their posts. He published books on the origins of the Universities of Oxford and Cambridge, and was known to have compiled catalogues of several libraries. He died early in 1658, according to a note in British Library, Harley MS 5898, 'of an extreme cold taken sitting in the University Library'.

By the time of his death the revival of Arabic studies in Europe was in full swing, and Langbaine was one of the scholars who had promoted them in this country. He had charge of the University's Arabic type, and he encouraged Edward Pococke, who held the Laudian chair in Arabic, to publish his *Specimen of the history of the Arabs* (*Specimen historiae Arabum*) and his edition and Latin translation of Abū l-Farāj (Barhebraeus)'s *History*. He also canvassed support for John Selden as a successor to Pococke in the Laudian chair. Selden owned the St Albans manuscript – Selden supra 24 – which has been the focus of much of the third lecture.

What has not been realised before, as far as I know, is that he compiled material from the Bodleian and other libraries in Oxford, to illustrate the history of the study of Arabic in England, from the beginnings up to his own time. This material is contained in a notebook marked with the astrological sign for Leo, now no. 12 in the Langbaine collection of the Bodleian Library.

He starts with Adelard of Bath, transcribing the opening of his *Natural Questions*, and underlining Adelard's mention of *Saraceni* and *studia Arabum* (Fig. 32). Then he refers to three translations from Arabic made by Adelard: the astronomical tables of al-Khwārizmī, Euclid's *Elements*, and the *Abbreviation of the introduction to astrology* of Abū Ma'shar. After mentioning Plato of Tivoli's translation of the canons to al-Battānī's astronomical tables, he transcribes the prefaces of two texts attributed to 'Robertus Anglicus': the first is the twelfth-century Robert of Ketton's translation of an introduction to astrology by al-Kindī, the second is the thirteenth-century Robert the Englishman's commentary on the *Sphere* of Sacrobosco. Then he quotes those portions of the dossier that Roger Bacon sent to Pope Clement IV that are relevant to the learning of Arabic. This is followed, quite appropriately, by a transcript of the rulings of the Council of Vienne concerning the teaching of Arabic, Greek, Hebrew and 'Chaldee'. Langbaine mentions a couple of instances of the execution of the ruling of the Council in Oxford, but only in respect to the teaching of Hebrew and of Chaldee. He goes on to transcribe the introduction of Daniel of Morley's *Philosophia*, in which, as we have seen, Daniel describes his visit to Toledo and his bringing of 'a precious multitude of books' from there to England.

Daniel's mention of Toledo as the place where the 'quadrivium' flourished prompts Langbaine to consider the meaning of 'quadrivium' and the origins of its study, quoting Alexander Nequam, Pseudo-Boethius's *De disciplina scholarium*, John of Salisbury's *Metalogicon*, John of Basingstoke's account of

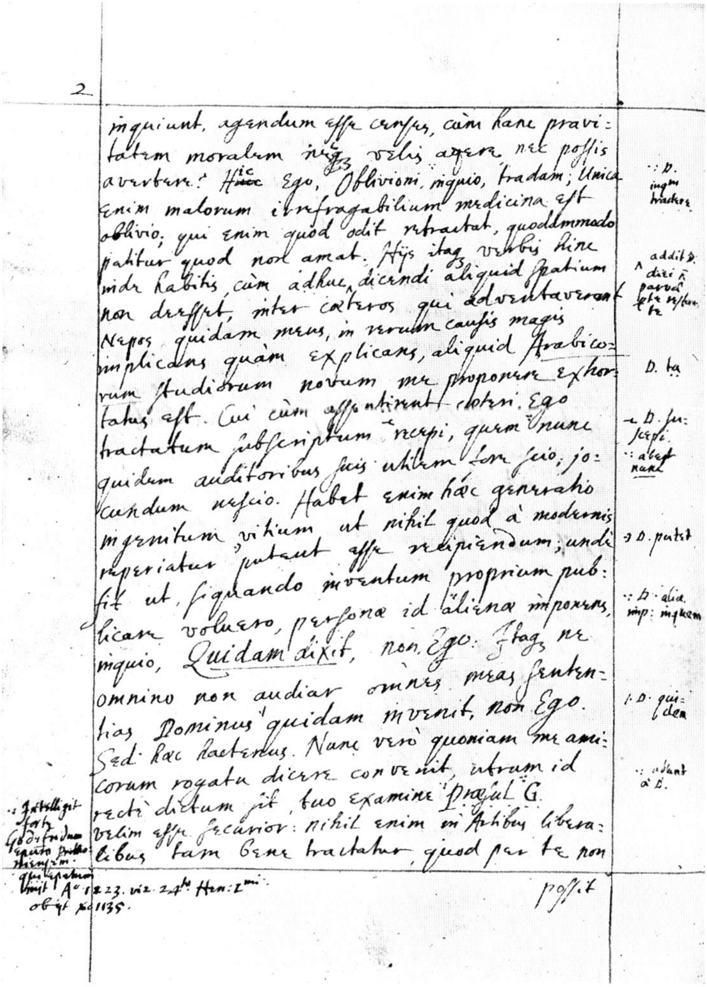

FIG.32. Oxford, Bodleian Library, Langbaine 12, p.2. Part of Langbaine's copy of the Adelard of Bath's prologue to his *Natural Questions*. Note that Langbaine has underlined *Arabicorum studiorum*.

Matthew Paris of St Albans, and more recent writers. Finally he adds:

> One may suspect that these words *trivium* and *quadrivium* have been taken from the Arabs. For not only does Egidius de Thebaldis imply that in the preface to (his translation of) the *Tetrabiblos* of Ptolemy (from Arabic), when he says, 'according to quadrivial science', but also, unless the Latin translation is faulty, Jacob Alkindi, an Arab who lived one century before Eutychius, in his work *On weather forecasting*, employs (the word) in the same sense in his preface, writing thus: 'Wise men knew that a man is not imbued in philosophy and does not know it before he can list weather forecasting among the subjects he knows, nor does he rise to that knowledge except after the four quadrivial sciences, which are the introduction to philosophy.'[214]

In surmising that the term 'quadrivium' came from the Arabs, Langbaine was not unique in his time. In fact his friend, fellow book-worm and Arabist, John Selden, says much the same. And it is with Selden's statement, which occurs in his translation and study of part of Eutychius's Arabic chronicle, concerning the patriarch of Alexandria, published in 1642 (to which Langbaine made reference in the passage just quoted), that I would like to end this series of lectures. Selden wrote:

> For the liberal and correctly taught sciences were formerly for a long time called by us [English] 'the studies of the Arabs' – the *studia Arabum*, as if called from the race and the places where they were then alone seriously cultivated. This is clear also from the preface to his *Natural Questions* of Adelard the monk of Bath (also called 'Athelard'), which he wrote when bringing the sciences back to England from the schools of the Arabs.[215]

Appendix

Didactic Rhymes and Jingles for Memorizing the Contents of the Quadrivium

In these lectures I have referred on several occasions to short rhymes and jingles which were used in the eleventh and twelfth centuries to memorize the contents of the quadrivium and to bring some enjoyment into learning it. This appendix provides a synopsis of these, and adds some related texts:

Arithmetic:
The numbers used in the algorism: 'Primus igin . . .'; see n.52 below.

The rules for calculating the church calendar (*computus*): Fulbert of Chartres, 'Annum Sol duodena . . .'; in several manuscripts; ed. F. Behrends in *The Letters and Poems of Fulbert of Chartres*, Oxford, 1976, pp.256–61.

Geometry:
The characters of the abacus: 'Ordine primogeno . . .'; see p.22 above.

The parts of the pound, the ounce and the *scripulus*: Fulbert of Chartres, 'Libra vel as ex unciolis constat duodenis . . .'; in many MSS, including Avranches, Bibliothèque municipale, 235, fol. 52r and Add. 17808, fol. 73r; in both manuscripts the full set of signs accompanies the verses; ed. F. Behrends in *The Letters and Poems of Fulbert of Chartres*, pp.254–7.

Music:
In music, mnemonics are generally sung. The best known of these is Guido d'Arezzo's composition of a melody to accompany a hymn of c.800 ('Ut queant laxis . . .') to serve as a mnemonic device for the notes in the scale (Guido d'Arezzo, *Epistola de ignoto cantu*, ed. M. Gerbert, *Scriptores ecclesiastici de musica sacra potissimum*, 3 vols, St Blasien, 1784, II, p.45). Hermann the Lame wrote three such mnemonics to remember musical intervals and to illustrate his own notation system: *E (e) voces unisonas aequat . . .*, *Ter tria sunt modi . . .*, and *Ter terni sunt . . .*, ed. Gerbert, ibid., II, 149–53; facsimiles in B. Stäblein, *Schriftbild der einstimmigen Musik*, Musikgeschichte in Bildern, III.4, Leipzig, 1975, Figs 90 and 95a-b. For anonymous verses, probably from the late 11th century, giving the names of the neums, with the neums written above ('Epiphonus strophicus/punctum porrectus oriscus . . .'), see M. Huglo, 'Les noms des neumes et leur origine', *Études Grégoriennes*, 1, 1954, p.57; these are comparable in form and purpose to the verses on the algorism 'Primus igin . . .' I am very grateful to the advice of Max Haas.

Astronomy:
The names of the fixed stars: 'Abdebaran Tauro . . .'; see p.5 above. The compass directions and elements: 'Oriens, meridies . . .; see p.10 above.

Rules for the use of astronomical tables: 'Saturni Iovis et Martis loca sic reperito . . .'; Arundel MS 377, fol. 74r and Oxford, Bodleian Library, Bodley 625, ed. F. S. Pedersen in 'A Twelfth-Century Planetary Theorica in the Manner of the London Tables', *Cahiers de l'Institut du moyen-âge grec et latin*, 60, 1990, pp.199–318 (see p.307).

Miscellaneous: 'Cullel.kauuekib . . .'; see pp.41–2 above.
'kulelach.uueli . . .'; see p.41 above.

NOTES

1 Paris, Bibliothèque nationale, n.a.l., 693, s. xiii, fol. 97r; the complete text has been edited in C. Burnett, *Magic and Divination in the Middle Ages*, Aldershot, 1996, article X, pp.8–17, where the illustrations of the marble hands are also reproduced.

2 Eadmund was the name of the East Anglian king and martyr whose body and name are preserved in Bury St Edmunds.

3 See N. Rogers, 'The Waltham Abbey Relic-List', in *England in the Eleventh Century*, ed. C. Hicks, Harlaxton Medieval Studies 2, Stamford, 1992, pp.157–81 and P. G. Schmidt, 'König Harold und die Reliquien von Waltham Abbey' in *Anglo-Saxonica*, eds K. R. Grinda and C.-D. Wetzel, Munich, 1993, pp.75–90.

4 Harley MS 978, fol. 116v: 'le livere al bon rei Edward'; from the Anglo-Norman version of Adelard's text, referred to by D. Evans in 'Adelard on Falconry', in *Adelard of Bath*, pp.25–7 (see p.26).

5 These books might have been part of the extensive donations given to Waltham Abbey by Harold. That there were precious books at the abbey soon after Harold's death is indicated by the fact that William the Conqueror upset the canons by removing '. . . four codices ornamented with gold, silver and jewels'; see Rogers, 'The Waltham Abbey Relic-List', p.163.

6 See D. Wasserstein, 'The Library of al-Ḥakam II al-Mustanṣir and the Culture of Islamic Spain', *Manuscripts of the Middle East*, 5, 1990–1, pp.100–5.

7 J. Samsó, *Islamic Astronomy and Medieval Spain*, Aldershot, 1994, article I, p.13.

8 See the articles published in *Physis*, 32, 1995: a special issue devoted to *The Oldest Latin Astrolabe*.

9 For the argument of this and the following paragraphs see Burnett, 'King Ptolemy and Alchandreus the Philosopher: The Earliest Texts on the Astrolabe and Arabic Astrology at Fleury, Micy and Chartres', (in press). Some of these chapters on surveying are grouped together in a compilation known since its edition by Nikolai Bubnov (*Gerberti opera mathematica*; Berlin, 1899, pp.310–64) as *Geometria incerti auctoris*. The most primitive forms of the first two texts (*De mensura astrolapsus* and *Sententie astrolabii*) and some further chapters from the third are edited in J. M. Millás Vallicrosa, *Assaig d'historia de les idees fisiques i matemàtiques a la Catalunya medieval*, I, Barcelona, 1931, pp.275–95 and 302–4.

10 The corpus was first analysed in detail by A. Van de Vyver, 'Les plus anciennes traductions latines médiévales (x^{e}–xie siècles) de traités d'astronomie et d'astrologie', *Osiris*, 1, 1936, pp.658–91. Van de Vyver identified six separate items of which two are reworkings of the first and main item: the

Liber Alchandrei Philosophi. I am grateful to David Juste for showing me his recent research on the corpus.

11 D. Pingree, 'The Preceptum Canonis Ptolomei', in *Rencontres de cultures dans la philosophie médiévale*, Louvain-la-Neuve–Cassino, 1990, pp.355–75.

12 F. Wallis, 'Images of Order in the Medieval *Computus*', in *Ideas of Order in the Middle Ages, Acta, 15, 1988*, Binghamton, N.Y., 1990, pp.45–68.

13 D. A. King, *Astronomy in the Service of Islam*, Aldershot, 1993.

14 A. Borst, *Astrolab und Klosterreform an der Jahrtausendwende*, Heidelberg, 1989.

15 Boethius, *De arithmetica*, ed. J.-V. Guillaumin, Paris, 1995, I, I.I.

16 P. Kunitzsch, 'Al-Khwarizmi as a Source for the *Sententie astrolabii*', in *From Deferent to Equant: A Volume of Studies in the History of Science in the Ancient and Medieval Near East in Honor of E. S. Kennedy*, ed. D. A. King and G. Saliba, New York, 1987, pp.227–36.

17 J. Vezin, 'Leofnoth: un scribe anglais à Saint-Benoît-sur-Loire', *Codices manuscripti*, 3, 1977, pp.109–20.

18 M. Mostert, *The Library of Fleury: A Provisional List of MSS*, Hilversum, 1989, p.107, says that it was probably written at Fleury and illuminated by an Anglo-Saxon scribe working there, and taken to England by Abbo and given to Ramsey at a later date.

19 *The Letters and Poems of Fulbert of Chartres*, ed. F. Behrends, Oxford, 1976, pp.xxvii–xxviii and 260–1.

20 C. Burnett, 'The Contents and Affiliation of the Scientific Manuscripts Written at, or Brought to, Chartres in the Time of John of Salisbury', in *The World of John of Salisbury*, ed. M. Wilks, Oxford, 1984, pp.127–60.

21 Borst, *Astrolab und Klosterreform*, p.68. An astronomical work by Abbo of Fleury (incipit: Studiosis astrologiae primo sciendum est . . .) was included in the Alchandrean corpus.

22 It was bought by the British Library from the Berlin bookseller, Asher, in 1849.

23 Add MS 17808, fols 73v–84v = Avranches, BM, fols 58r–73v.

24 This text is edited in Burnett, 'King Ptolemy'. Significant is the fact that where the Corpus Christi and British Library manuscripts diverge, the scribe of the Avranches manuscript has the reading of the British Library manuscript in his text, but has copied the variant readings of the Corpus Christi manuscript into the margin.

25 A scribe has pointed to these lines as 'versus': the compass directions and elements are each followed by the last three and a half feet of a hexameter.

26 See Fig. 3. Other English manuscripts are Sloane MS 2030, of the twelfth century (see Fig. 4), and Arundel MS 339 and Bodleian Library, Ashmole 369, both of the thirteenth century.

27 William of Malmesbury, *Gesta regum Anglorum* (written 1114–23 with additions in 1140), ed. W. Stubbs, London, 1887, II, c. 167. The latter is

probably a variant or corruption of the title 'Proportiones competentes in astrorum industria', one of the components and the Alchandrean corpus.

28 Edited F. Behrends, *The Letters and Poems of Fulbert of Chartres*, pp.254–5.

29 See p.14 below.

30 Richer, *Historiae, apud* Bubnov, *Gerberti opera mathematica*, p.381.

31 William of Malmesbury, *Gesta regum Anglorum* , ed. W. Stubbs, II, c. 167: 'abacum certe primus a Sarracenis rapiens, regulas dedit, quae a sudantibus abacistis vix intelliguntur'.

32 W. Bergmann, *Innovationen im Quadrivium des 10. und 11. Jahrhunderts*, Sudhoffs Archiv, Beiheft 26, Stuttgart, 1985, pp.175–215.

33 D. A. King, 'The Earliest Known European Astrolabe in the Light of Other Early Astrolabes', *Physis*, 32, 1995, pp.359–404 (see pp.371–2). The numerical values of the Latin letters are based on those of the equivalent *maghrebi* (Western) Arabic letters.

34 E.g., that of Stephen of Pisa; see R. W. Hunt, 'Stephen of Antioch', *Medieval and Renaissance Studies*, 6, 1950, pp.172–3.

35 MS San Lorenzo del Escorial, codex Vigilianus, lat. d.1.2, fol. 9v: 'Scire debemus [in] Indos subtilissimum ingenium habere, et ceteras gentes eis in arithmetica et geometrica et ceteris liberalibus disciplinis concedere. Et hoc manifestum est in nobem (*sic*) figuris quibus designant unumquemque gradum cuiuslibet gradus quarum hec sunt forma (*sic*).'

36 See G. Beaujouan, 'The Transformation of the Quadrivium' in *'Par raison de nombres'*, Aldershot, 1991, article III, and Burnett, 'The Instruments which are the Proper Delights of the Quadrivium: Rhythmomachy and Chess in the Teaching of Arithmetic in Twelfth-Century England', *Viator*, 28, 1997, (in press).

37 Bernelinus, *Liber abaci*, *apud* Bubnov, *Gerberti opera mathematica*, p.383: '. . . a domino papa Gerberto quasi quaedam seminaria breviter et subtilissime seminatus. Quod si tibi taedium non esset harum fervore Lotharienses expetere quos in his ut cum maxime expertus sum florere.'

38 In the early twelfth century Raoul of Laon sees the mathematics of his time as stemming from two sources, Gerbert d'Aurillac and Hermannus Contractus of Reichenau; see Bubnov, *Gerberti opera mathematica*, p.389.

39 M. Folkerts, *'Boethius' Geometrie II, ein mathematisches Lehrbuch des Mittelalters*, Wiesbaden, 1970, pp.105–6.

40 Fols 84v–85v. This text begins 'Rationes abaci numeri videntur ratione formari et ex ipso naturaliter institui', and does not appear to be extant elsewhere. This text does not indicate the form of the abacus and whether counters with Arabic numerals were used.

41 A. Peden, 'Science and Philosophy in Wales at the Time of the Norman Conquest: A Macrobius Manuscript from Llanbadarn', *Cambridge Medieval Celtic Studies*, 2, 1981, pp.21–45 (see p.25).

42 J. Barrow, 'A Lotharingian in Hereford: Bishop Robert's Reorganisation of the Church of Hereford 1079–1095', in *Medieval Art, Architecture and Archaeology at Hereford*, ed. D. Whitehead, The British Archaeological Association, Leeds, 1995, pp.29–49.
43 See previous note.
44 A. Cordoliani, 'L'Activité computistique de Robert, évêque de Hereford', *Mélanges offerts à René Crozet*, ed. P. Gallais and Y. T. Rion, Poitiers, 1966, I, pp.33–40.
45 William of Malmesbury, *Gesta pontificum Anglorum*, §164, ed. N. E. S. A. Hamilton, London and Cambridge, 1870, p.300.
46 C. H. Haskins, *Studies in the History of Medieval Science*, 2nd edn, Cambridge, Ma., 1927, p.333: 'Non tua te mathesis, presul Rodberte, tuetur, /Non annos aliter dinumerans abacus'.
47 Richer, *Historiae*, as cited by Bubnov, *Gerberti opera mathematica*, p.381: 'notas omnem numerum significantes'.
48 William of Malmesbury, *Gesta pontificum*, p.313.
49 Emmanuel Poulle is sceptical as to whether the 'astrolabium' he refers to was an astrolabe rather than simply a chart to convert unequal hours to equal hours: 'La littérature astrolabique latine jusqu'au xiiie siècle', *Physis*, 32, 1995, pp.227–37 (see p.231).
50 According to C. W. Hollister, *Monarchy, Magnates and Institutions in the Anglo-Norman World*, London, 1986, p.312, the sons and nephews of several of Henry's key administrators were students at the school of Laon.
51 Adelard, *Regulae abaci*, ed. B. Boncompagni in *Bullettino di bibliografia e di storia delle scienze matematiche e fisiche*, 14, 1881, pp.1–134. The immediate sources of this text have not yet been investigated, but it includes a passage which is clearly indebted to the *Geometry II* of Pseudo-Boethius; see M. Folkerts, 'Adelard's Versions of Euclid's *Elements*', in *Adelard of Bath*, pp.60–1.
52 The same poem directly follows Fulbert's poem on the divisions of the pound in Avranches, Bibliothèque municipale 235, fol. 52r (= MS A). The following edition is based on both manuscripts. Paris, BN, lat. 15119, fol. 40r (= P) places the relevant abacus numerals in front of each of the verses but omits the title; both copies place the description of '0' before that of '9'. The same names (without the zero) appear in two lines of verse in the late twelfth-century manuscript Cambridge, Trinity College, R.15.16, fol. Av – here they accompany the algorism, and the Hindu-Arabic numerals are written over the relevant names: 'Primus igin, andras, ormis, quarto subit arbas / Post quimas, iermas, zenis, zenoma, zelentis'.
53 zelentis A.
54 sypos A.
55 vocatur P.
56 A reference to the shape of the sign for 'zero'.

57 *Constantine the African and 'Alī ibn al-'Abbās al-Mağūsī: The* Pantegni *and Related Texts*, eds C. Burnett and D. Jacquart, Leiden, 1994. For the date of Constantine's death see the article by Francis Newton in this volume: 'Constantine the African and Monte Cassino: New Elements and the Text of the *Isagoge*', pp.16–47 (see p.23)

58 *De eodem et diverso*, ed. H. Willner, BGPM, 4.1, Münster, 1903, pp.33-4. 'quendam philosophum Graecum, qui prae ceteris artem medicinae naturasque rerum disserebat, sententiis praetemptarem'.

59 M. R. James, *The Ancient Libraries of Canterbury and Dover*, Cambridge, 1903, p.59; see B. Lawn, *The Salernitan Questions*, Oxford, 1963, p.19.

60 Marius is linked to Alfano by Gottfried of Viterbo, whose teacher Marius was; see Dagmar Gottschall, 'Marius Salernitanus und Gottfried von Viterbo', *Sudhoffs Archiv*, 75 (1991), 111–3 (p.113). He should not be identified with Petrus Alfonsi; see Burnett, 'The Works of Petrus Alfonsi: Questions of Authenticity', *Medium Ævum*, 66, 1997, pp.42-79.

61 Opinions concerning the date of this manuscript vary; see Newton, 'Constantine the African and Monte Cassino', p.17, n. 5.

62 Two manuscripts are listed in the late twelfth- or early-thirteenth-century catalogue of the abbey: see M. R. James, *On the Abbey of S. Edmund at Bury*, Cambridge, 1895, p.28; the Bury MS, Cambridge, Trinity College, R.13.34 (James catalogue, no. 906) may be one of them.

63 N. R. Ker, *Medieval Libraries of Great Britain*, London, 1964, p.85.

64 The Arabic text has not been identified.

65 J. Wilcox and J. M. Riddle, 'Qusṭā ibn Lūqā's *Physical Ligatures* and the Recognition of the Placebo Effect', *Medieval Encounters*, I, 1995, pp.1–50.

66 Roger Bacon, *Epistola de secretis operibus artis et naturae, et de nullitate magiae*, in *Fr. Rogeri Bacon Opera quaedam hactenus inedita*, ed. J. S. Brewer, I, London, 1859, pp.528. I am grateful for the advice of Roberto Casazza.

67 An example is provided in M. H. Green, 'The Development of the *Trotula*', *Revue d'histoire des textes*, 26, 1996, pp.119–204, where the twelfth-century work on women's medicine, *De cura mulierum*, is shown to include both references to Salernitan women and Salernitan masters, and English names for medical conditions and *materia medica* (see pp.136–7).

68 Warin, prior (from 1173) and abbot (1183–95) of St Albans had studied at Salerno with his brother Matthew and two other monks who entered the monastery at the same time. Other heads of houses who had spent time in Southern Italy were Adalbold of St Edmunds and Robert of St Frideswides.

69 Leiden, Bibliotheek der Rijksuniversiteit, Voss. Lat. Q. 84, fols 12v–16v + Paris, Bibliothèque nationale, lat. 2389, fols 65–81v + Leiden, ibid., BPL 121.

70 The Waltham Abbey list is edited in M. R. James, 'MSS from Essex Monastic Libraries', *Transactions of the Essex Archaeological Society*, new series, 21, 1937, pp.34–62 (see pp.42–3).

71 See n. 5 above.

72 'Quod regalis generis nobilitas artium liberalium studio se applicat, valde assentior. Quod rerum gubernandarum occupatio ab eodem animum non distrahit, non minus ammiror. Intelligo itaque te, Henrice, cum sis regis nepos, a Philosophia id plena animi percepisse nota. Ait enim beatas esse res publicas si aut philosophis regende tradantur aut earum rectores philosophie adhibeantur. Huius rationis odore ut infantia tua semel inbuta est in longum servat, quantoque gravius exterioribus honeratur, tanto ab eisdem diligentius se subtrahit. Inde fit ut non solum ea que Latinorum scripta continent intelligendo perlegas, sed et Arabum sententias super spera et circulis stellarumque motibus intelligere velle presumas. Dicis enim ut in domo habitans quilibet, si materiam eius vel compositionem, quantitatem et qualitatem, situm et distinctionem ignoret, tali hospitio dignus non est. Sic qui in aula mundi natus atque educatus est, si tam mirande pulcritudinis rationem scire negligat post discretionis annos, ea indignus atque, si fieri posset, eiciendus est. His a te frequenter ammonitus, licet meis non confidam viribus, tamen ut nobilitati philosophiam uno nostre etatis exemplo coniungam, postulationi tue pro posse meo dabo operam. De mundo igitur eiusque distinctione quod Arabice didici Latine subscribam'; adapted from the edition of B. G. Dickey, in 'Adelard of Bath: An Examination Based on Heretofore Unexamined Manuscripts', unpublished Ph.D dissertation, University of Toronto, 1982, pp.147–8.

73 *Gesta Stephani*, ed. and transl. K. R. Potter, London, 1955, p.148: 'receptusque cum gloria ab omnibus qui audito illius adventu undecumque confluxerant, cumulatissime in omni provincia a singulis fuit honoratus utpote eorum dominus, et munerum impensione largissime donatus'.

74 This is indicated *inter alia* by the mention of Adelard's opinions and his 'intelligence' (*ingenium*) in the margins of the *commentum*-version of Euclid's *Elements* in several manuscripts, and in the margins of Boethius's *De musica* in Oxford, Trinity 47; see M. Folkerts, 'Adelard's Versions of Euclid's *Elements*' in *Adelard of Bath*, pp.55–68 (see p.63), and n. 92 below. For other references to his pupils see Burnett, '*Algorismi vel helcep*', n. 110 below, pp.231–4.

75 Richard of Poitiers, quoted in C. Baswell, *Virgil in Medieval England*, Cambridge, 1995, p.178, who discusses Peter's Troy poem.

76 W. L. Warren, *Henry II*, London, 1973, pp.38–9.

77 See nn. 80 and 81 below.

78 A late medieval preface to the twelfth-century *Moralium dogma philosophorum* asserts that, according to some people, the work was written by William the teacher of Henry, the Count of Anjou's son: '[hoc opus] fecit

. . . secundum quosdam magister Guilhelmus, qui Henricum filium comitis Andegavie de Campania Gallica instruebat' (*Das Moralium Dogma Philosophorum des Guillaume de Conches*, ed. J. Holmberg, Uppsala, 1929, p.6). William's authorship of the *Moralium dogma philosophorum* (or *De honesto et utili*) is disputed; more trust can be put in the fact that several manuscripts include a dedication to 'Henricus'. It may be significant that the work occurs alongside Adelard's *De eodem et diverso* and *Natural Questions* in the Waltham Abbey list.

79 See A. Speer, *Die entdeckte Natur: Untersuchungen zu Begründungsversuchen einer "scientia naturalis" im 12. Jahrhundert*, Leiden, 1995, chapter 3.

80 William of Conches, *Dragmaticon*, printed as *Dialogus de substantiis physicis . . . a Vuilhelmo Aneponymo philosopho*, ed. G. Gratarolus, Strasbourg, 1567, p.4: 'tibi cum filiis tuis aliquid quod ad scientiam pertineat scribere proposuimus'.

81 Ibid., pp.3–4: 'In te tamen et in filiis tuis aliquid spei consistit quos non ut alii ludo alearum sed studio literarum tenera aetate imbuisti cuius odorem diu servabunt, iuxta illud Horatii: "Quo semel est imbuta etc." '

82 Brian Lawn, *The Salernitan Questions*, pp.51–3, lists and discusses the questions and answers in Adelard's *Natural Questions* that have equivalents in William's *Philosophia*; see also Italian translation, Naples, 1969, *nota aggiunta B*, pp.232–3.

83 A. Clerval, *Les Écoles de Chartres au Moyen-Age*, Chartres, 1895, p.180. Whether John of Salisbury's studies with William of Conches between 1138 and 1141 took place at Chartres or Paris is disputed (see K. S. B. Keats-Rohan, 'The Chronology of John of Salisbury's Studies in France: A Reading of *Metalogicon*, 2.10', *Studi Medievali*, 3rd series, 28, 1987, pp.193–203), but there is no doubt that William was in Chartres as a student of Bernard, and the latest research has shown that the *Heptateuchon* was made at Chartres: see P. Stirnemann, 'Où ont été fabriqués les livres de la glose ordinaire dans la première moitié du xiie siècle?' in *Le xiie siècle: mutations et renouveau en France dans la première moitié du xiie siècle*, ed. F. Gasparri, Paris, 1994, pp.257–302 (see pp.275–6).

84 Both Lawn (*The Salernitan Questions*, p.52, n. 3) and Dorothy Elford ('Developments in the Natural Philosophy of William of Conches: A Study of his *Dragmaticon* and a Consideration of its Relationship to the *Philosophia*', unpublished PhD dissertation, Cambridge, 1983, pp.233–7), show how passages in the *Dragmaticon* are even closer to the *Natural Questions* than equivalent passages in the *Philosophia*.

85 M. A. Rouse and R. H. Rouse, ' "Potens in Opere et Sermone": Philip, Bishop of Bayeux, and His Books', in their *Authentic Witnesses: Approaches to Medieval Texts and Manuscripts*, Notre Dame, Indiana, 1991, pp.33–59 (see p.46, n. 50).

86 H. Hine, 'The Manuscript Tradition of Seneca's *Natural Questions*', *Classical Quarterly*, 30, 1980, pp.183–217.

87 Rouse and Rouse, '"Potens in Opere et Sermone"', pp.53–4.

88 Daude de Pradas, *Le Roman dels Auzels Cassadors*, ed. A. H. Schutz, Columbus, Ohio, 1945, v. 1930.

89 Salzburg, St Peter Stiftsbibliothek, a.V.2. The combination was known to, and exploited by, Daniel of Morley, see below, p.63.

90 Baswell, *Virgil in Medieval England*, pp.44–6; U. Rees, *The Cartulary of Haughmond Abbey,* Cardiff, 1985, no. 411.

91 Other glosses to Boethius's *De arithmetica*, and on diagrams in Euclid's *Elements*, include Arabic words in transcription.

92 Trinity 47, fol. 99r: 'nota quia duo tractus incausti secundum Alvredum sunt ut sit inter meses pagina significans tonum ut inter alias, sed Adelardus id inprobat per superiorem notam'. This gloss and the previous one, which presumably gives Adelard's view, are printed in *Adelard of Bath*, p.83.

93 For Adelard's literal translation of the *Elements*, the 'commentum'- and other Arabic-Latin versions see M. Clagett, 'The Medieval Latin Translations from the Arabic of the *Elements* of Euclid', *Isis*, 44, 1953, pp.16–42, and C. Burnett, 'The Latin and Arabic Influences on the Vocabulary Concerning Demonstrative Argument in the Versions of Euclid's *Elements* Associated with Adelard of Bath', in *Aux origines du lexique philosophique européen*, ed. J. Hamesse, Louvain-la-Neuve, 1997, (in press).

94 See P. E. Dutton in his edition of Bernard of Chartres, *Glosae super Platonem*, Toronto, 1991, pp.70–96.

95 It is unlikely that the manuscript was ever presented to a royal patron since it is incomplete.

96 For a full account of Petrus's life and work see Burnett, 'The Works of Petrus Alfonsi'.

97 Oxford, Bodleian Library, Auct. F.1.9, fol. 96r: 'Sententia Petri Ebrei, cognomento Anphus, de dracone, quam dominus Walcerus, prior Malvernensis ecclesie, in Latinam transtulit linguam'. This text is edited by J.-M. Millás Vallicrosa, in 'La aportación astronómica de Pedro Alfonso', *Sefarad*, 3, 1943, pp.87–97.

98 MS Cambridge, University Library, Ii.VI.11, s. xiv, fol. 95 (heading to Petrus's *Dialogus contra Iudaeos*).

99 R. Mercier, 'Astronomical Tables in the Twelfth Century', in *Adelard of Bath*, pp.87–118, see pp.99–100.

100 'Ne igitur opus quod Arabica lingua dicitur Ezich quodque vir subtilissime scientie, Elkaurezmus vocabulo, de cursu .vii. planetarum subtilissime composuit et seriatim digessit, oblivioni tradatur, Arabici anni primus mensis ubi et qua die vel qua hora diei incepit notare disposuit'. I am grateful to Patrick McGurk for allowing me to quote from his new edition of the

Chronicle of John of Worcester. John of Worcester also describes the causes of a solar eclipse in terms reminiscent of both Walcher's *Sententia . . . de dracone* (ed. Millás Vallicrosa, p.87) and Petrus Alfonsi's description of the phenomenon in his version of al-Khwārizmī's tables (Lambeth Palace, 67, fol. 92v and Oxford, Corpus Christi College 283, fol. 142r): see *Chronicle*, ed. Weaver, pp.37 and 61.

101 The possibility that Adelard himself brought manuscripts from the Principality of Antioch should not be ruled out, especially since he is probably to be identified with the 'Antiochenus' referred to by John of Seville and Limia as an earlier translator of Thābit b. Qurra's *Book on Talismans* (*Liber prestigiorum*).

102 The contrast between Adelard's references to 'latina scripta' and 'magistri' who are Arabic is explored in Burnett, 'Adelard of Bath and the Arabs', in *Rencontres de cultures dans la philosophie médiévale*, eds M. Fattori and J. Hamesse, Louvain-la-Neuve and Cassino, 1990, pp.89–108.

103 For a description of this text, and translated excerpts from it, see Burnett, *Magic and Divination in the Middle Ages*, Aldershot, 1996, I, pp.9–13.

104 *Liber prestigiorum*, edition in preparation based on MS Lyon, Bibliothèque municipale, 328, fols 70–74 and Vatican, Pal. lat. 1401: 'O fons honoris, gaudium et lux mundi, miscete amores, spiritus, horum scientia miscendi utentes, virtute in illos maxima adiuti et potentia elmelik (regis) elkeudduc (sancti) elhaiedemi (immortalis) potentiaque eius qui circulos movet, dans eis supra mundum hunc inferiorem noram (lucem) et eian (illuminationem)'.

105 The verses are written as continuous sentences in the manuscript. I have divided the lines to show the rhythm and rhyme-scheme.

106 I have corrected the obvious manuscript error 'otari.a'.

107 The incorrect word division in the roman transcription might be accounted for by the scribe's (perhaps subconscious) attempt to show where the syllables divide, especially in the case of the first *punctum* of the first phrase.

108 In the second phrase this vowel-rhyme is achieved at the expense of Classical Arabic syntax ('hu' instead of 'hā') and a feminine plural form ('qumna') seems to be used instead of the correct feminine singular ('qāma'), which would not fit the rhythm.

109 The examples have been taken from Brugge, Stadsbibliotheek 529; see the list of Arabic words in transcription in H. L. L. Busard, *The First Latin Translation of Euclid's Elements Commonly Ascribed to Adelard of Bath*, Studies and Texts 64, Toronto, Pontifical Institute of Mediaeval Studies, 1983, pp.391–6, supplemented by Burnett, review of Busard's book, in *Archives internationales d'histoire des sciences*, 35, 1985, pp.475–80.

110 The text is edited and discussed in C. Burnett, '*Algorismi vel helcep decentior est diligentia*: the Arithmetic of Adelard of Bath and his Circle', in

Mathematische Probleme im Mittelalter: Der latinische und arabische Sprachbereich, ed. M. Folkerts, Wolfenbüttel, 1996, pp.221–331 (see pp.234–44 and 261–97).

111 In the process of copying, it is apparent that an 's' has been omitted and there has been confusion between the 'long-s' and the 'f' (which differ only by a small cross-stroke) at the beginning of the word.

112 A list of these Arabic terms is given in Burnett, 'Adelard of Bath and the Arabs', p.103, n. 52.

113 'Unde fit ut naturali sedis positione domus philosophica esse perhibeatur. Illic enim et omnia semina sponte proveniunt et indigene tam morum honestatem quam verborum veritatem modis omnibus illesam custodiunt, solique Deo principaliter, stellarum vero numinibus secundario obnoxii, in communi omnia ponentes feliciter degunt solamque nature et rationis viam sequentes. Cum aliquem cuiuslibet legis virum in commerciis suis vident, proverbio utuntur tali: "aiekadeb", id est "cave bestiam". Quibus, si Arabes sequimur, eam patriam habitare datum est in qua primus homo, omnibus planetis preter Mercurium in regnis suis existentibus, Creatore volente statuque celi ad generationem applicante, exortus est'; adapted from *De opere astrolapsus*, ed. Dickey, pp.169–70.

114 *Encyclopedia of Islam*, second edn, II, Leiden, 1965, s.v. Dābba (A. Abel).

115 Plato's doctrine of the Philosopher King could have been known to Adelard through Lactantius's *Divinae institutiones*, III.21 (PL 6, 418A-B), or Cicero, *Ad Quintum fratrem*, epist. 1. I am grateful to Robert Ziomkowski for this information.

116 See J. D. North, 'Some Norman Horoscopes', in *Adelard of Bath*, pp.147–61. These horoscopes have been written on a fold of parchment tacked into British Library, Royal MS App. 85; they would appear to be the original documents of the astrologer, who is not named. I am now inclined to attribute them not to Adelard, but rather to an astrologer working in London, Stephen's stronghold – perhaps Robert of Chester, who drew up astronomical tables for London; see below, p.58.

117 See Mercier, 'Astronomical Tables in the Twelfth Century', pp.107–112, and, more fully, in 'The Lost Zij of al-Ṣūfī in the Twelfth Century Tables for London and Pisa', in *Lectures of the Conference of As-Sûfi and Ibn-an-Nafis*, Jordan, 1987, pp.38–72.

118 Y. T. Langermann, 'Some Astrological Themes in the Thought of Abraham ibn Ezra', in *Rabbi Abraham ibn Ezra: Studies in the Writings of a Twelfth-Century Jewish Polymath*, eds I. Twersky and J. M. Harris, Cambridge, Ma., 1993, pp.28–85 and B. R. Goldstein, 'Astronomy and Astrology in the Works of Abraham ibn Ezra', *Arabic Sciences and Philosophy*, 6, 1996, pp.9–21.

119 These neighbouring cities were very important for their Jewish communities, the former being referred to as 'the little Jerusalem', the latter the seat

of the 'Jewish kings of Narbonne'; see *Encyclopedia Judaica*, s.vv. 'Béziers' and 'Narbonne'.

120 Professor Tzvi Langermann has kindly told me that it is commonly believed that Ibn Ezra wrote one version in 1146 and a revision in 1148.

121 J. Jacobs, *Jews in Angevin England*, London, 1893, gives the testimonies that he was in London at least in May and December 1158.

122 Mercier, 'The Lost Zij of al-Ṣūfī', p.52 writes that 'it is not clear why [Abraham] should have been interested in the longitude of Angers'.

123 The terms 'toletane (figure)' and 'indice f(igure)' are found on the fly-leaf of a twelfth-century manuscript of astronomical/astrological works, Munich, Bayerische Staatsbibliothek, clm 18927 (fol. 1r) where they are written alongside the relevant sets of numerals; see Figure 1a in R. Lemay, 'The Hispanic Origin of Our Present Numeral Forms', *Viator*, 8, 1977, pp.435–62. The 'toletane (figure)' could also be described as 'Mozarabic', since they first occur in manuscripts written in Mozarabic script and the Mozarabs were an important element of the Toledan population. Both forms of the numerals are given in one manuscript of Abraham's Hebrew work on the algorism (*Sefer ha-mispar*, in MS Paris, BN, hébreu 1052). I owe this reference to Tzvi Langermann.

124 The first work has lost its beginning, which suggests that at least another quire of 8 folios preceded.

125 The only heading in most of the Latin manuscripts is 'Dixit Abraham Iudaeus'; one MS calls the work 'Abrahismus'.

126 *El libro de los fundamentos de las Tablas astronómicas de R. Abraham Ibn Ezra*, ed. J. M. Millás Vallicrosa, Madrid and Barcelona, 1947; Millás discusses the date of the work on p.16.

127 Rudolph's work is unpublished, but has been discussed briefly by Kunitzsch, *Glossar der arabischen Fachausdrücke in der mittelalterlichen europäischen Astrolabliteratur*, Göttingen, 1983, pp.485–6. His presence in Béziers on 24 April, 1144, is indicated by the only dated and located example in his text: Cotton, Vespasian A II, fol. 36v: 'Verbi gratia, anno domini .mcxliiii. Biteris in Gotia iuxta mare mediterraneum . . . xxiiii. die aprilis'.

128 Keys are found in the above-mentioned MS Munich, Bayerische Staatsbibliothek, clm 18927, fol. 1r, and in MSS Bodleian, Digby 40, fol. 88v and Selden supra 26, fol. 106r; in the latter manuscript the 'figure toletane' are also written above the 'figure indice' in the text.

129 Harley MS 5402, fol. 69v is virtually a summary (with the substitution of Lucca for Pisa, and the longitude 34° for 33°) of the first three chapters of the *Tractatus magistri Habrahe* in Arundel MS 377, fol. 36v–37r.

130 Abraham bar Ḥiyya, the Jewish exegete, and author of astronomical, astrological and trigonometrical works, working in Barcelona in the 1130s, shares with Ibn Ezra the distinction of creating a language of scientific discourse in Hebrew; see J.–M. Millás Vallicrosa, *Estudios sobre historia de la*

ciencia española, Barcelona, 1949, pp.219–62. He specifically mentions that he is making translations from Arabic into Hebrew for the French (*Galli*); his astronomical tables are extant in Latin in a twelfth-century English manuscript: Cambridge, University Library, Hh.VI.8, vol. 1, fols 41–77: see Mercier, 'Astronomical Tables', p.103. The Latin works that he wrote in collaboration with Plato of Tivoli are most completely represented in the twelfth-century manuscript, Oxford, Bodleian, Digby 51, which also includes a translation by Robert of Ketton, Rudolph of Bruges's work on the astrolabe, and an unidentified arithmetical work which uses the 'figure indice'. Bar Ḥiyya is not unconnected with Ibn Ezra, since some manuscripts of his tables include some tables and notes ascribed to Ibn Ezra (information from Tzvi Langermann).

131 A third manuscript of the twelfth century that appears once to have contained both the Pseudo-Ptolemaic *Iudicia* and the works of Raymond of Marseilles was Chartres, Bibliothèque nationale, 213, destroyed in the Second World War (see Burnett, 'The Contents and Affiliation of the Scientific Manuscripts Written at, or Brought to, Chartres', pp.135–6 and 140). The Chartrian connection is entirely compatible with what has been suggested for the itinerary of these works.

132 Further astronomical material was added in blank spaces in the manuscript and on fly-leaves, including the observations of eclipses at the abbey of St Trond (OSB; now in Belgium) in 1287 and 1288; there are no indications of the manuscript's earlier provenance.

133 This is immediately followed by verses on how to use astronomical tables, in the tradition of those already quoted on the fixed stars on the astrolabe, the divisions of the pound and the abacus; see Appendix.

134 For Robert's terminology see the table of equivalent terms in Mercier, 'Astronomical Tables' (= M), pp.116–8; among the terms used by Robert which recur in the margins of Arundel MS 377 are 'residui' M19, 'linee numeri' M29 and 'coequatio', cf. M30.

135 For Robert's involvement with the tables of Pisa see Mercier, 'Astronomical Tables', p.109 and 'The Lost Zij of al-Ṣūfī', pp.40–1, where the problems of chronology are discussed. The arguments for the attribution of the *commentum*-version of Euclid's *Elements* are set out by the editors of that text, H.L.L. Busard and M. Folkerts (*Robert of Chester's (?) Redaction of Euclid's* Elements, *the so-called Adelard II Version*, 2 vols, Basel-Boston-Berlin, Birkhäuser, 1992, I, pp.22–31).

136 Daniel of Morley, *Philosophia*, ed. G. Maurach, *Mittellateinisches Jahrbuch*, 14, 1979, pp.204–55; see sections 64–7 and 70, pp.223–5.

137 This is demonstrated in C. Burnett, 'The Institutional Context of Arabic-Latin Translations of the Middle Ages: a Reassessment of the "School of Toledo"', in *Vocabulary of Teaching and Research Between Middle Ages and Renaissance*, ed. O. Weijers, Turnhout, 1995, pp.214–35 (see pp.221–3).

Hermann collaborated with Robert and was the teacher of Rudolph of Bruges.

138 Peter the Venerable, *Epistola ad Bernardum Clarævallis*, ed. J. Kritzeck, *Peter the Venerable and Islam*, Princeton, New Jersey, 1964, p.212: '. . . interpretantibus scilicet viris utriusque linguæ peritis, Rotberto Ketenensi de Anglia, qui nunc Pampilonensis ecclesiæ archidiaconus est, Hermanno quoque Dalmata, acutissimi et litterati ingenii scolastico, quos in Hispania circa Hiberum astrologicæ arti studentes inveni'.

139 See C. Burnett, 'Antioch as a Link between the Culture of the East and the West in the Twelfth and Thirteenth Centuries', to be published in the proceedings of the conference *L'Occident et le Proche-Oriente au temps des crusades: traductions et contacts scientifiques entre 1000 et 1300*, ed. A. Tihon, I. Draelants and B. Van den Abeele, Louvain (in press).

140 This is where Hermann completed his major work, the *De essentiis*, according to the colophon: 'De essentiis liber Hermanni Secundi explicit, anno domini millesimo centesimo quadragesimo tertio Byterri (*v.l.* Biternis) perfectus'. I do not find convincing the arguments for identifying the place of writing with the coastal region of Guipuzcoa (in the Basque region) given by M. Alonso in his edition of Hermann of Carinthia, *De essentiis*, *Miscelánea Comillas*, 5, Santander, 1946, pp.7–107 (pp. 14 and 23) and developed by R. Lemay in his edition of Abū Ma'shar al-Balhī [Albumasar], *Liber introductorii maioris ad scientiam judiciorum astrorum*, 9 vols, Naples, 1995–6, VII, pp.83–4.

141 See note 127 above.

142 Mercier points out ('The Lost Zij of al-Ṣūfī', p.49) that in the *Book of the Foundations of the Astronomical Tables* 'the longitude of Angers is determined by a solar eclipse observed at Bordeaux, which is on the same meridian'. This may suggest that Ibn Ezra was preparing the text for the Duke of Anjou on his way north from Béziers, which would have passed through Toulouse and Bordeaux.

143 Cotton MS Vespasian, A II, fol. 40v: 'Ut ait philosophorum sibi contemporaneorum HABRAHAM magister noster egregius quo dictante et hanc dispositionem astrolabii conscripsimus' (Fig. 27).

144 The identification is not without problems, which are such that Richard Southern made two scholars out of them (*Robert Grosseteste: The Growth of an English Mind in Medieval Europe*, 2nd edn, Oxford, 1992, pp.xlvii–xlix).

145 E.g., (1) Hermann of Carinthia, who is not recorded in Spain after 1143, but to whom a Greek-Latin translation of the *Almagest* made in Palermo in ca. 1160 is attributed, or (2) Rudolph of Bruges, or (3) a Latin scholar from Antioch, such as Stephen of Pisa, who might have introduced the 'figure indice' into Abraham's works, or (4) more than one Latin scholar. Mercier ('The Lost Zij of al-Ṣūfī', p.51) shows that the system of transliteration of Arabic words in the *Book of the Foundations of the Astronomical Tables* is sig-

nificantly different from that of the introduction to the Pisan tables in the Fitzwilliam manuscript.

146 I take up the term that is often encountered for the wise men, expert in the secular arts, who advised the king or another nobleman; for examples see C. Burnett, 'Magister Theodore, Frederick II's Philosopher', in *Federico II e le nuove culture*, Atti del XXXI Convegno storico internazionale, Todi, 9–12 ottobre 1994, Spoleto, 1995, pp.225–85. For Henry's support of literature and learning see Haskins, 'Henry II as a Patron of Literature', in *Essays in Medieval History Presented to Thomas Frederick Tout*, ed. A. G. Little and F. M. Powicke, Manchester, 1925, pp.71–7; and P Dronke, 'Peter Blois and Poetry at the Court of Henry II', in id., *The Medieval Poet and His World*, Rome, 1983, pp.281–339.

147 Haskins ('Henry II as a Patron of Literature', p.73) refers to Pipe Roll 31 Henry II p.146: 'Nova placita et nove conventiones per . . . Walterum Map et Rogerum clericum de Hereford'; and Pipe Roll 33 Henry II, p.55: 'Deulebeneie Judeus de Risinges debet x *l.* pro recto de debitis suis versus Amalricum de Bellafago . . . et Danielem de Merlay'.

148 *Dialogus de scaccario*, ed. and trans. C. Johnson, with corrections by F. E. L. Carter and D. E. Greenaway, Oxford, 1983, p.xxiii: 'The justiciar, head of the *Curia regis* and of the Exchequer in the King's absence, may be regarded as corresponding to the Steward (*Dapifer*), the Count Palatine of the Empire, who was also the chief judge. According to Richard FitzNigel, author of the *Dialogus* (pp.57–9), the King "had such a high opinion of [Robert], that he appointed him Justiciar, head not only of the Exchequer, but of the whole kingdom" '.

149 This version is found in Royal MS 12.E.XXV and Bodleian Library, Digby 57; see D. Crouch, *The Beaumont Twins*, Cambridge, 1986, p.209 on Robert's learning.

150 Royal MS 15.C.XIV, fol. 1r: 'reputans mecum incongruum valde fore [de] tot et tantarum regionum dominum et rectorem ignorare partes orbis cuius non minime parti dominaris'; partial edition, K. Rück, Sitzungsberichte der Kaiserlichen bayerischen Akademie der Wissenschaften, philos.-philol. Kl. 1902, Munich, 1902, pp.195–285 (p.265).

151 Haskins, *Studies*, p.169. Haskins's further suggestion that Henry's courtier Thomas Brown was the 'Qaid Barrūn' who had been head of the diwan, or Arabic treasury, of Roger II, the king of Sicily (p.189), has now been discounted (J. Johns, 'The Greek Church and the Conversion of Muslims in Norman Sicily?', in *Byzantinische Forschungen*, 221, 1995, pp.132–57; see p.139), though Thomas Brown had been in Sicily and connections between the two countries were close: see Haskins, 'England and Sicily', *English Historical Review*, 26, 1911, pp.433–47 and 641–65 (see pp.438–43).

152 This translation with another Hebrew version of the *Natural Questions* is edited by H. Gollancz in *Dodi ve-Nechdi*, London, 1920.

153 Jacobs, *Jews in Angevin England*, pp.25–7; Jacobs claims that Solomon lived in London in ca. 1150. See also *Starrs and Jewish Charters Preserved in the British Museum*, ed. and transl. I. Abrahams, H. P. Stokes and H. Loewe, 3 vols, Cambridge and London, 1930–2, II, pp.cxvi–cxvii. The interpretation of the seal is unclear; the Arabic title may simply attest to Solomon's high rank.

154 M. Beit-Arié, *Hebrew Manuscripts of East and West: Towards a Comparative Codicology*, The Panizzi Lectures 1992, London, 1993, p.8; cf. the more detailed description in id., *The Only Dated Medieval Hebrew Manuscript Written in Enland (1189 CE) and the Problem of Pre-Expulsion Anglo-Hebrew Manuscripts*, London, 1985, pp.33–5 and Plates 6–7. Here Beit-Arié surmises that the Jewish creditor may have been the same Solomon ben Isaac.

155 See p.40 above. Hugo of Santalla, working in Tarazona, and in close contact with Hermann and Robert, also acknowledged the superiority of the Arabs in the science of the stars, writing that 'it befits us to imitate the Arabs especially, for they are as it were our teachers and precursors in this art'; Burnett, 'A Group of Arabic-Latin Translators Working in Northern Spain in the mid-twelfth Century', *Journal of the Royal Asiatic Society*, year 1977, pp.62–108 (see p.90).

156 Robert of Ketton, preface to translation of al-Kindī, *Iudicia*, Bodleian, Digby 51, fol. 55r: 'eum quem commodissimum et veracissimum inter astrologos iudicem vestra quam sepe notavit diligentia'.

157 *Metalogicon*, 4.6, ed. B. Hall, Turnhout, 1991, p.145.

158 John of Salisbury. Letter no. 272, to Baldwin of Exeter (April–May, 1168): 'Cum autem dominum papam blanditiis et promissis dejicere non praevalerent, ad minas conversi sunt [*sc. the messengers of the king*], mentientes quod rex eorum Noradini citius sequeretur errores, et profanae religionis iniret consortium, quam in ecclesia Cantuarensi Thomam pateretur diutius episcopari'; *Letters*, ed. W. J. Millor and C. N. L. Brooke, II, Oxford, 1979, pp.560–1.

159 Daniel refers to two characters – Titius and Seius – often used in examples in Roman Law books.

160 Daniel of Morley, *Philosophia*, ed. G. Maurach, pp.204–55 (see p.212).

161 R. W. Southern, 'From Schools to University' in *The History of the University of Oxford*, ed. J. I. Catto, Oxford, 1984, pp.1–36 (see p.12). Daniel's failure to reach Northampton and his stopping at Oxford, if true, would also be symbolic of the decline of Northampton as a potential or actual *studium generale* and the ascendancy of Oxford: see A. B. Cobban, *The Medieval English Universities: Oxford and Cambridge to c. 1500*, Berkeley and Los Angeles, 1988, pp.29–30 and 33.

162 The arguments for Daniel meeting John in Oxford are given in A. Birkenmajer, 'Eine neue Handschrift des "Liber de naturis inferiorum et superiorum" des Daniel von Merlai', in his *Études d'histoire des sciences et de*

la philosophie du moyen âge, Studia Copernicana, 1, Wrocław, Warszawa and Kraków, 1970, pp.45–52. However, up to now, no scholar, as far as I know, has suggested that John of Oxford had any role in encouraging the establishment of a *studium generale* at Oxford. One would imagine that, considering he was a close friend and adviser of the king, the academic body at Oxford would have valued his support. The importance of Oxford for King Henry II, and the nature of the king's support of the university are pointed out by Southern, 'From Schools to University', p.14, and Cobban, *The English Universities*, p.33.

163 The testimonies and *magistri* are listed in Southern, 'From Schools to University'.

164 *Philosophia*, ed. Maurach, p.215.

165 See p.32 above.

166 Alfarabi, *Über den Ursprung der Wissenschaften (de ortu scientiarum)*, ed. C. Baeumker, BGPM, 19, Münster-i.W., 1918, p.20.

167 The *De ortu scientiarum* even includes a literal translation of the Arabic declaration of faith 'lā llāh illā Allāh' – 'there is no God but Allah' – in the phrase 'deus praeter quem non est deus'; ibid., p.23.

168 Ibid., p.20.

169 Daniel, *Philosophia*, beginning of Book II, ed. Maurach, p.228: 'It is fair then, that, since you are not ignorant of those opinions of the philosophers about the supercelestial things which are current among the Latins, you should not disdain to listen carefully to the irrefutable reasonings of the Arabs, because, although it is perhaps dangerous to imitate their teaching in some respects, it will none the less be useful to know about those things which are proved to be erroneous, so that, when they are known beforehand, they are easier to attack, and an intelligent man can more easily take precautions for himself.'

170 Adelard, *Natural Questions*, prologue, ed. Müller, BGPM, 31.2, Münster-i.W., 1934, p.1: to prevent being criticized for the Arabic views that he propounds he says to his detractors: 'Quidam dixit, non ego'.

171 *Philosophia*, ed. Maurach, p.129.

172 Here I must express my gratitude to Oliver Gutman who has prepared an edition of this text under my supervision: '*Liber celi et mundi*: Introduction and Critical Edition', D. Phil., Oxford, 1996.

173 M. Alonso, 'Hunayn traducido al Latin por Ibn Dawud y Domingo Gundisalvo', *Al-Andalus*, 16, 1951, pp.37–47.

174 See O. Gutman, 'On the Fringes of the *Corpus Aristotelicum*: The Pseudo-Avicenna *Liber celi et mundi*', *Early Science and Medicine*, 2, 1997, pp.1–20 (see p.16).

175 Ed. Maurach, p.230, section 102.

176 See Gutman, 'On the Fringes', pp.11–13.

177 Dominicus Gundissalinus, *De divisione philosophiae*, ed. L. Baur, BGPM, 4.1, Münster-in-W., 1903, p.20.

178 The most significant of these are Paris, Bibliothèque nationale, lat. 6443 and 14700, and Toledo, Bibl. Capitul. 47.15.

179 See C. Burnett, '*Magister Iohannes Hispanus*: Towards the Identity of a Toledan Translator', in *Comprendre et maîtriser la nature au moyen âge: mélanges d'histoire des sciences offerts à Guy Beaujouan*, Geneva, 1994, pp.425–36.

180 Gerson D. Cohen, *Ibn Daud Sefer Ha-Qabbalah*, London, 1967, preface. For the decisive effect of the expulsion on Jewish life and culture see B. Septimus, *Hispano-Jewish Culture in Transition: The Career and Controversies of Ramah*, Cambridge, Ma., 1982, p.2.

181 These texts are edited by Birkenmajer, 'Avicennas Vorrede zum "Liber Sufficientiae" und Roger Bacon', in his *Études d'histoire des sciences et de la philosophie du moyen âge*, pp.94–101, and by S. Van Riet in Avicenna, *Liber de anima*, Louvain and Leiden, 1972, pp.3–4.

182 *Philosophia*, ed. G. Maurach, pp.244–5: 'Girardus Tholetanus, qui Galippo mixtarabe interpretante Almagesti latinavit'.

183 K. Sudhoff, 'Die kurze "Vita" und das Verzeichnis der Arbeiten Gerhards von Cremona', *Archiv für Geschichte der Medizin*, 8, 1914, pp.73–82; English translation by Michael McVaugh in *A Source Book in Medieval Science*, ed. E. Grant, Cambridge, Ma. 1974, pp.35–8.

184 MSS Avranches 221 and 232 (from Mont St-Michel); see Burnett, 'The Introduction of Aristotle's Natural Philosophy into Great Britain: A Preliminary Survey of the Manuscript Evidence', in *Aristotle in Britain during the Middle Ages*, ed. J. Marenbon, Turnhout, 1996, pp.21–50 (see p.33). That the translation of the *Ethica vetus* (as well as the Greek-Latin translation of the *De generatione et corruptione*) should be ascribed to Burgundio is demonstrated by F. Bossier, 'La cheminement d'un traducteur: L'élaboration du vocabulaire philosophique chez Burgundio de Pise', in *Aux origines du lexique philosophique européen: L'influence de la "latinitas"*', ed. J. Hamesse, Louvain-la-Neuve, 1997, (in prose); Bossier substantiates a claim made by R. Durling in 'The Anonymous Translation of Aristotle's *De generatione et corruptione*', *Traditio*, 49, 1995, pp.320–30.

185 R. W. Hunt, 'English Learning in the Late Twelfth Century', *Transactions of the Royal Historical Society*, 4th series, 19, London, 1936, pp.19–42 (see p.36).

186 The same work, with the title 'Liber Aristotilis de expositione bonitatis pure' appears in the list of translations by Gerard of Cremona, drawn up by his students, and the terminology of the translation does suggest Gerard's authorship (see R. Taylor. 'Remarks on the Latin Text and the Translator of the *Kalâm fi mahd al-khair/ Liber de causis*', *Bulletin de philosophie médiévale*, 31, 1989, pp.75–83). However, some scholars have claimed that

another version or revision was due to Gundissalinus (A. Pattin, 'Over de schrijver en de vertaler van het *Liber de causis*', *Tijdschrift voor Filosofie*, 23, 1961, pp.323–33 and 503–26). In any case, the title 'Metaphysica Avendauth' begs an explanation, of which the one advanced here (that it came into England on the coat-tails of the *De ortu scientiarum* and *Liber celi et mundi*), is only one possibility. The *De causis* was not in the Mont St-Michel manuscripts.

187 Henry of Avranches, *apud* D. A. Callus, 'Introduction of Aristotelian Learning to Oxford', *Proceedings of the British Academy*, 29, 1943, pp.229–81 (see p.242).

188 The only exception is a confused reference to the Arabic-Latin translation of Aristotle's *De caelo*, under the title 'Physica', in Johannes Blund, *Tractatus de anima*, ed. D. A. Callus and R. W. Hunt, Oxford, 1970, p.3, section 8.

189 These translations and their accompanying glosses are most extensively surveyed in L. Minio-Paluello, *Opuscula: The Latin Aristotle*, Amsterdam, 1972.

190 Gerard's *socii* certainly thought that Gerard already knew Aristippus's translation, for they write in the list of his works: 'Liber Aristotilis meteororum tractatus III, quartum autem non transtulit, eo quod sane invenit eum translatum'. The 'sane' gives the statement the sense that 'he *surely* knew that it had been translated'; Sudhoff, 'Die kurze "Vita"', p.78.

191 MS Selden supra 24, fol. 109r. Alfred's name is given here as 'Aurelius' which I would interpret as a Classical equivalent for the Germanic 'Alvredus' rather than a corruption. Alfred's contribution to the booklets making up Selden supra 24 could also have extended to the interlinear alternate readings in Burgundio's translation of the *De generatione et corruptione*: these come from Gerard of Cremona's Arabic-Latin translation; see J. Judycka, preface to her edition of *De generatione et corruptione*, Aristoteles Latinus, 9.1, Leiden, 1986, p.xxv. Again it should be emphasised that these additions are not in the Mont St-Michel manuscript of the work (Avranches, BM, 232).

192 Alfred of Sareshel's *Commentary on the* Metheora *of Aristotle*, ed. J. K. Otte, Leiden, 1988, p.37.

193 *Commentary on the* Metheora, ed, Otte, p.51: 'Israelita celeberrimus et modernorum philosophorum precipuus'.

194 L. Thorndike, *Michael Scot*, London, 1965, C. Burnett, 'Michael Scot and the Transmission of Scientific Culture from Toledo to Bologna via the Court of Frederick II Hohenstaufen', *Micrologus*, 2, 1994, pp.101–26, and F. J. Hernández, 'La Fundación del Estudio de Alcalá de Henares', *En la España Medieval*, 18, pp.61–83 (see p.68).

195 Only the Middle Commentary on the fourth book of the *Meteora* was translated, but even this did not have a wide diffusion and apparently was

not used in the manuscripts containing the 'Oxford Gloss' (see n. 203 below). This area needs further research.

196 See R. A. Gauthier, 'Notes sur les débuts (1225–40) du premier Averroïsme' in *Revue des sciences philosophiques et théologiques*, 66, 1982, pp.321–74 and C. Burnett, 'The Introduction of Arabic Learning into British Schools', *The Introduction of Arabic Philosophy into Europe*, ed. C. E. Butterworth and B. A. Kessel, Leiden, 1994, pp.40–57.

197 This 'English tradition' is well-documented by Southern, in *Robert Grosseteste*.

198 Southern, 'From Schools to University', p.36.

199 Grosseteste, *Commentary on the* Physics *of Aristotle*, ed. R. C. Dales, Boulder, 1963, see p.xiv.

200 The prologue to the *Rhetoric* (written before 1256) has been reproduced from Paris, BN, lat. 16673 by J. Ferreiro Alemparte in 'Hermann el Alemán, traductor del siglo XIII en Toledo', *Hispania sacra*, 35, 1983, pp.9–56 (see pp.11-12).

201 C. Burnett, '*Magister Iohannes Hispalensis et Limiensis* and Qusṭa ibn Lūqā's *De differentia spritus et animae*: a Portuguese Contribution to the Arts Curriculum?' *Mediaevalia. Textos e estudos*, 7–8 (1995), pp.221–67 (see pp.249–51); it is referred to in Bartholomeus Salernitanus's commentary to the *Ysagoge* of Johannitius in MS Winchester 24, f. 33v, see D. Jacquart, 'Aristotelian Thought in Salerno', in P. Dronke, *Twelfth-Century Western Philosophy*, ed. P. Dronke, Cambridge, pp.407–28 (see p.426).

202 One of the few definite dates in Adam's intellectual career is in the document that indicates that 'on 22 February 1244 Magister William of Solers noted payment of twelve *soldi* for 22 *peciae* of Adam's *libri naturales*'; J. A. Weisheipl, 'Science in the Thirteenth Century', in *The History of the University of Oxford*, I, pp.435–69 (see p.463).

203 Aristotle, *Physica. Translatio vetus*, ed. F. Bossier and J. Brams, Aristoteles Latinus, VII.1, 2 fascicles, Leiden and New York, 1990, p.lv, C. Burnett and A. Mendelsohn, 'Aristotle and Averroes on Method in the Middle Ages and Renaissance: the "Oxford Gloss" to the *Physics* and Pietro d'Afeltro's *Expositio Proemii Averrois*' in *Method and Order in Renaissance Philosophy of Nature: The Aristotle Commentary Tradition*, ed. E. Kessler, et al., Aldershot, 1998, (in press), and S. Donati, 'Physica I, 1: L'interpretazione dei commentatori inglesi della *Translatio vetus* e loro recezione del commento di Averroe', *Medio Evo*, 21, 1995, pp.75–255.

204 This note is edited as Appendix II in C. Burnett, 'The Introduction of Aristotle's Natural Philosophy', p.46.

205 These are: Harley MS 3487, and Royal MS 12.G.II, 12.G.III and 12.G.V.

206 Alfred is called 'commentator' by Grosseteste, referring to Alfred's *De plantis*, and by Roger Bacon, referring to his *Meteora* commentary; see M. Grabmann, 'Die Aristoteleskommentatoren Adam von Bocfeld und Adam

von Bouchermefort, die Anfänge der Erklärung des "neuen Aristoteles" in England', in *Mittelalterliches Geistesleben*, II, Munich, 1936, pp.138–82 (see p.142).

207 E.g. in Paris, Bibliothèque nationale, lat. 14700, see d'Alverny, *Avicenna Latinus: Codices*, Louvain-la-Neuve and Leiden, 1994, p.281; a manuscript in the Walters Library in Baltimore states that Alkindi wrote a commentary on the *De generatione et corruptione* and Alfred corrected it and divided it into chapters: see *Aristoteles Latinus: Codices*, 2 vols, ed. G. Lacombe, Rome, 1939–55, I, pp.237–8; this could be true.

208 Where he spent the ten years 1247 to 1257 is disputed; he refers to seeing books both in Paris and in Oxford: see Weisheipl, 'Science in the Thirteenth Century', pp.454–5.

209 D. Salman, 'Algazel et les latins', *Archives d'histoire doctrinale et littéraire du moyen âge*, 10, 1936, pp.103–27.

210 Roger Bacon repeated his criticisms on several occasions; see his *Opus tertium*, chapter 25, ed. J. S. Brewer, *Fr. Rogeri Bacon Opera Quædam Hactenus Inedita*, I, London, 1859, p.91, *Compendium studii philosophiae*, chapter 8, ibid., pp.471–2 (William of Moerbeke's name added), and *Opus maius*, Pars Tertia, *De utilitate grammaticae*, ed. J. H. Bridges, Oxford, Clarendon Press, 1897, 2 vols, I, pp.66–9 and 81.

211 *Compendium studii*, c. 8.

212 *Opus maius*, Pars Tertia, *De utilitate grammaticae*, p.67.

213 See biography in *Dictionary of National Biography*, s.v., and *A Summary Catalogue of Western Manuscripts in the Bodleian Library at Oxford*, ed. F. Madan, II, p.990. For the background, see now G. J. Toomer, *Eastern Wisedome and Learning: the Study of Arabic in Seventeenth-Century England*, Oxford, 1996.

214 MS Langbaine, 12, p.94: 'Utrum hoc vocabulum Trivii et Quadrivii ab Arabibus deductum suspicari licet, non modo enim Aegidius de Tebaldis (*in margin*: Ms Digby 179) in præfatione ad Ptolomæi Quadripartitum *Secundum Quadrivialem scientiam* dicens, eò respexit, sed et nisi versio latina erronea Jacobus Alkindi Arabs ipse Eutychio seculo uno antiquior in De impressionibus et aeris accidentibus (*in marg.* MS Digby 68) eodem sensu usurpat in præfatione sic scribens: Et sciverant sapientes quod homo non est imbutus in philosophia, nec scit eam usque quo possit (*in marg*: impress. mendosè (ut plurima) . . . *followed by seven letters difficult to read*) dinumerare cum scientia impressiones superiores, nec ascendit ad illam scientiam nisi post scientias Quadriviales, quæ sunt introitus ad philosophiam.'

215 'Nam & Scientiæ Liberales ritèque institutæ, diù ante vocari solebant à Nostris *Studia Arabum & Arabica Studia*, veluti denominata à gente ac locis ubi tunc solùm seriò colebantur. Id etiam liquet ex Præfatione Adelardi Monachi Bathoniensis, Athelardi item dicti, in Quæstiones suas Naturales quas ex Arabum Scholis redux in Angliam conscripsit': *Eutychii Patriarchæ*

Orthodoxorum Alexandrini . . . Ecclesiæ suæ Origines. Ex eiusdem Arabico nunc primùm typis edidit ac Versione et Commentario auxit Ioannes Seldenus, London, 1642, p.156. This reference was kindly pointed out to me by Gerald Toomer who is preparing a book on Selden.

Manuscripts